WHAT ROUGH BEAST?

WHAT ROUGH BEAST?

IMAGES OF GOD IN THE HEBREW BIBLE

David Penchansky

Westminster John Knox Press
Louisville, Kentucky

Scripture quotations from the New Revised Standard Version of the Bible are copyright © 1989 by the Division of Christian Education of the National Council of the Churches of Christ in the U.S.A. and are used by permission.

Grateful acknowledgment is made to the following for permission to reprint copyrighted material:
"The Well-Dressed Man with a Beard," from *Collected Poems* by Wallace Stevens. © 1942 by Wallace Stevens. Reprinted by permission of Alfred A. Knopf, Inc.
Tropic of Cancer, by Henry Miller. © 1961. Reprinted by permission of Grove/Atlantic, Inc.
"The Second Coming," by W. B. Yeats. Reprinted with the permission of Simon & Schuster from *The Poems of W. B. Yeats: A New Edition,* edited by Richard J. Finneran. © 1924 by Macmillan Publishing Company, renewed 1952 by Bertha Georgie Yeats. *Selected Poetry,* by Gerard Manley Hopkins, © 1996. By permission of Oxford University Press.
Fidelity: Five Stories, by Wendell Berry. Published by Pantheon Books © 1992.

Book design by Sharon Adams
Cover design by LMNOP
Cover illustration: © 1999 PhotoDisc, Inc.

First edition
Published by Westminster John Knox Press
Louisville, Kentucky

This book is printed on acid-free paper that meets the American National Standards Institute Z39.48 standard. ♾

PRINTED IN THE UNITED STATES OF AMERICA

99 00 01 02 03 04 05 06 07 08—10 9 8 7 6 5 4 3 2 1

Library of Congress Cataloging-in-Publication Data

Penchansky, David.
    What rough beast? : images of God in the Hebrew Bible / David Penchansky.
            p.   cm.
    Includes bibliographical references.
    ISBN 0–664–25645–7 (alk. paper)
       1. God—Biblical teaching.   2. Bible.   O.T.—Theology   I. Title
    BS1192.6.P46   1999
    231'.4—dc21   99–27859

To my children Maia and Simon

Obscurity I do and will try to avoid so far as is consistent with excellences higher than clearness at first reading.

—*Gerard Manley Hopkins,*
preface to *Selected Poetry*

CONTENTS

Introduction

Is it beyond our capacity to imagine a really and entirely loving image of God? The Western traditions of religion, most notably Judaism, Christianity, and Islam, claim such a God, but never without considerable subtlety. Within the pages of the Hebrew Bible we find expressions of a different image of God, one much more sinister. I believe these are genuine expressions of an Israelite sensibility, an Israelite theology, and not primitive holdovers of an earlier, less monotheistic faith. They are truly Israelite, not vestiges of an earlier age and a different people.

I like to ask my classes, when we are examining a new text, to do two things for me. I do not try to justify the activity. I just ask them to do it. First, I ask them to read these texts as if God is a character in a story. (Throughout this book I will refer to the Israelite God as YHWH, the four consonants of the divine name the Israelites used to refer to their God.) Second, I ask: "If all you knew about God you knew from this passage, how would you describe the divine being?" In this book I try to follow the same principle. I have isolated six narratives that depict God negatively.[1] They produce troubled readings when forced to conform to the traditional verities regarding the nature of God. God in these passages is rough, violent, unpredictable, liable to break out against even his most faithful believers without warning.

That provided the source for my title, *What Rough Beast?* William Butler Yeats's famous poem "The Second Coming" envisions a divine procession, both powerful and frightening in its destructive potential. The entire line reads:

> And what rough beast, its hour come round at last,
> Slouches towards Bethlehem to be born?[2]

This same beast is "moving his slow thighs" and has a "gaze blank and pitiless as the sun." There have always been those who regard God not as a comforting but rather as an unfair and frightening figure, one that threatens. God's presence then becomes something to flee, something to escape.

I have always sensed great power and truth in these difficult passages, truths which perhaps lie at the underbelly of belief, in the same place as doubts and skepticism, although that is not what these stories represent. They represent rather a *different* statement of faith than that of the traditional formulations, traditional (I suspect) even at the time they were written. This different faith did not accept that the universe balanced out with fairness—the just rewarded and the wicked punished. This was a world in which the innocent suffer and YHWH, the God of Israel, is the culprit who inflicts these wrongs.

My first effort to address these issues gave attention to a single book of the Hebrew Bible, the book of Job.[3] In it I suggested that the portrait of deity was ironical and deliberately deconstructive. The writing suggested that this was an *undesirable* portrayal of God, one that inevitably, when put to the test, led to absurdity—as exemplified first by the friends who blame Job for his misfortune, and second by YHWH's paltry efforts to defend himself and restore Job's fortunes.

This *is* a negative portrayal of deity (or, a portrayal of a negative diety), and the sympathetic figure is Job, not YHWH. However, there is no uniformity in the theology of negative deity in the Hebrew Bible. By that I mean that the portrayal of God in Job differs significantly from negative portrayals in other parts of the Bible. The six I have chosen, briefly, are: (1) Genesis 2–3, popularly known as the Garden of Eden story. In this narrative, YHWH Elohim (as he is called) places a tree of divine knowledge in the middle of the garden and then forbids the humans to eat it. They eat it, and nothing happens in the way YHWH had foretold. Such a God is *insecure*. (2) Second Samuel 6, in which Uzzah, trying to prevent the ark of the covenant from falling in the dirt, is struck dead. Such a God is *irrational*. (3) Second Samuel 24, wherein YHWH, angry at Israel, incites David to sin and then uses that as an excuse to punish Israel, killing many thousands— a *vindictive* God. (4) Leviticus 10, in which the two sons of the high priest in Israel offer "strange incense" to YHWH, and he burns them to death. Here YHWH is *dangerous*. (5) Exodus 4:24–26, where YHWH, having commissioned Moses to liberate the Israelites from Egyptian slavery, meets that same Moses on the road to Egypt and tries to kill him, prevented from doing so only by quick thinking by Zipporah (Moses' wife). Zipporah experienced God as *malevolent*. (6) Second Kings 3, in which a band of children mock the prophet Elisha, and he calls down hideous and painful deaths upon them—an *abusive* God.

In each of these passages I will ask the question, If all I knew of God I knew from this passage, how would I then understand the divine being? In such an examination, I will not be uncovering outmoded ideas, beliefs long since "grown out of" by the evolving Israelite sensibility. Rather, I suspect, beliefs and theologies expressed in these stories provide (1) an important key to how the Israelites understood their God and how they processed important personal and national events, making them understandable within their religious context, and (2) an important source of religious/theological reflection in our present day. By this I mean that in the face of the experience of war and atrocity in the twentieth century (now mercifully coming to a close), perhaps we need to revisit the notion of a dangerous God, perhaps even an evil God. That there is ample religious precedence for such a move in the Hebrew Bible should give us courage in our speculations. But more than that, also, these stories provide a *structure,* a shape in which we may understand our own century, and our individual experiences of suffering within it.

I feel impressed by the *chutzpah* of these ancient writers, who treat God without the utmost respect and seriousness to which God is accustomed. Sometimes the boldness of their portrayal frightens me, but their intellectual honesty, their willingness to look into the very face of the abyss, and do so with courage and wit, and a certain ironic twinkle in the eye, makes their portrayals not only tolerable but desirable. I sense a similar sentiment in Henry Miller, whose profane stance rivals both the Yahwist and the Deuteronomist:

> This is not a book, in the ordinary sense of the word. No, this is a prolonged insult, a gob of spit in the face of Art, a kick in the pants of God, Man, Destiny, time, Love, Beauty, what you will. I am going to sing for you, a little off key perhaps, but I will sing. I will sing while you croak, I will dance over your dirty corpse. . . .[4]

YHWH the Monster:
The *Insecure* God
(Genesis 3)

Lo! ye believers in gods all goodness, and in man all ill, lo you!
See the omniscient gods oblivious of suffering man; and man,
though idiotic, and knowing not what he does, yet full of the
sweet things of love and gratitude.

Herman Melville, Moby Dick

Monsters with "great staring eyes" inhabit the nightmare regions of fantasy. In the Hebrew Bible great sea creatures and land giants lay waiting in the chaos just outside the imposed order of God's creation. Sometimes, however, the divine figure itself functions as monster.[1] In Genesis 2–3 the god is called YHWH/Elohim, usually translated "LORD God." We may learn a great deal about this figure, but only if first we ignore what other parts of the Bible say about God. Most of the traditions (academic and confessional) believe God to be good and limitless in knowledge and power. Therefore, any biblical story that implies otherwise must be either ignored or aggressively interpreted so as to force it to agree with more acceptable theological views. The Genesis 2–3 story, however, has not been ignored by any of the traditions, ancient or modern. It is thick with conflicting interpretations, agglomerated as it has passed from community to community. While most of the interpretations assume the spotless reputation of YHWH/Elohim, in this story there are monstrous aspects to the divine figure that should not be ignored.

THE MAGICAL TREES

YHWH/Elohim put two special trees in the middle of the Garden of Eden. The trees have names (the Tree of the Knowledge of Good and Evil; the Tree of Life), although it is in no way clear what the names actually mean. The serpent states that upon eating from the Tree of the Knowledge of Good and Evil, the woman will "be like *'elohim* [God or gods], knowing good and evil" (Gen. 3:5). The tree apparently imparts a divine breadth of knowledge.[2] The woman observes that the tree is able to make one wise (Gen. 3:6). Although two different phrases are used ("be like God, knowing good and evil," and "able to make one wise"), here they both speak of knowledge such as that possessed by the *'elohim*, a class of beings to which YHWH/Elohim belongs, and over which he rules. According to YHWH/Elohim, the other tree, the Tree of Life, imparts divine immortality.[3] If the humans ate from that tree as well, they would have divine knowledge *and* divine immortality and would therefore be virtually indistinguishable from the *'elohim*.[4]

So why did YHWH/Elohim place these trees right in the middle of the garden, presumably not a hidden place but rather a most prominent location? After he plants the trees, he delivers a very stern warning to the man: "On the *very* day you eat from the tree, you will *instantly* die."[5] Why would he place the trees (the text switches in a confusing manner between one tree and two[6]) in such a prominent place if he didn't want the humans to eat their fruit?

It Is a Test

According to this understanding, YHWH/Elohim placed these trees in the garden for the express purpose of providing the first humans a test of their obedience to divine commands. The importance of the trees lay not in whatever magical powers they might have possessed, but rather in their having been chosen as a site of testing. Through the test YHWH/Elohim would discover the extent of human loyalty. Further, there exists the possibility that the humans might benefit from the test as well, advancing to some new level of responsibility in the divine training program. If the humans did not eat the fruit, they would pass the test.

Certainly there are other passages in which God tests humans, most prominently the "Akedah," the offering of Isaac (Genesis 22). In both cases (the Garden of Eden and the Akedah) a difficult, incomprehensible, and counterintuitive command must be obeyed so as to prove devotion to God. Abraham proves his devotion because he willingly offers his own child as a human sacrifice. The first humans fail to prove their devotion when they disobey the prohibition and eat from the Tree of Knowledge.[7] If we see the prohibition as a test, that would explain why the divine threat (" . . . you will die *instantly*") was never carried out. Just as God never intended to allow Abraham to destroy his son, he never meant to carry out the punishment against the first humans.

However, there is no testing language in the Garden of Eden passage. In Genesis 22 the narrator declares that "God *tested* Abraham" and the divine messenger reacts to the conclusion of the test with great joy: "Now I know that you fear God." There is no such framing device in the Garden of Eden story that would clearly suggest that this is a test. But if it is not a test, why did YHWH/Elohim give the humans access to the trees? That the Christian, and to some extent the Jewish, tradition makes of this story an exquisite testing myth does not exhaust its possibilities. Such a reading might not even represent a historically early reading, or even a best or most useful reading. I can think of two other possible readings:

YHWH/Elohim *Wanted* the Humans to Eat the Fruit, but Couldn't Tell Them

Everyone knows that in many folk stories the protagonist must break free from the confines of her parents so that she might find her destiny. In these stories, a wise parent recognizes the necessity that children must rebel in order to establish their separate identities.[8] In such a way, YHWH/Elohim created a controlled environment in which the humans (his children, so to speak) might rebel and establish their independence. Although he made them believe that he did not want them to eat the fruit, in fact that was his intention all along. The whole setting served as an elaborate scheme to advance the first humans, because (in this explanation) humans can only establish their independence if they disobey God, the authority figure.

There are problems with understanding the story this way. YHWH/Elohim appears genuinely upset when he finds out that they ate the fruit. "Then Yahweh/Elohim said, 'See, the man has become like one of us, knowing good and evil; and now, he might reach out his hand and take also from the tree of life, and eat, and live forever' " (Gen. 3:22). When YHWH/Elohim discussed the situation with the other *'elohim*, they considered issues of damage control. Probably, no one felt happy about the way things turned out. It is therefore hard to accept that YHWH/Elohim *intended* the humans to eat the forbidden fruit, when all his actions indicate otherwise.

YHWH/Elohim Did Not Anticipate That the Humans Would Disobey Him

In order to take this interpretation seriously, one has to drop any notion that YHWH/Elohim has all power and all knowledge. If the fruit of the two trees gave nourishment and divine abilities to the *'elohim*, perhaps YHWH/Elohim placed them in the garden for his and the others' convenience. A firm threat, he thought, was sufficient to keep the humans away. It didn't turn out as planned, and the *'elohim* resorted to "plan B" by driving the humans out of the garden, denying them access to fruit from the Tree of Life, and thus keeping them in a position inferior to that of the divine beings.

YHWH's placement of the trees was a colossal blunder, one he tried to rectify by banishing the couple. YHWH forbade them to eat the fruit, under threat of death, but this turned out to be an empty threat. And when the threat didn't work, he ejected them from the garden. I find this reading most helpful in understanding the theology of the passage. It fits most fully with the portrayal of the serpent in the narrative.[9]

THE SERPENT

For a long time I have taught that the serpent is not to be identified with subsequent notions of Satan or the devil. Israel distinguished itself from the surrounding nations by its strict monotheistic ideas. YHWH, the Israelite God, shares his power with no other god or divine being. Notions of rival cosmic powers such as devils come from foreign influence, and (it is implied) are not worthy of Israel. And does not the narrator take great effort to establish that the serpent is not a supernatural power, but rather one of the creatures that were made by YHWH/Elohim?[10] "The serpent was more crafty [*arum:* clever, shrewd] than any other wild animal that YHWH/Elohim had made" (Gen. 3:1). However, in many ways the serpent distinguishes himself from the other beasts and resembles a supernatural creature, strongly akin to the figure of Satan in the opening chapters of the book of Job.[11] This "creature" can talk, is clever/shrewd, and appears privy to the secrets of the divine council. Whatever additional knowledge might be gained by eating the magical fruit, the serpent seemed to have already. The serpent makes statements that provide important information about the tree and about the character of YHWH/Elohim. The serpent reveals the secrets that YHWH/Elohim wants to conceal.

YHWH/Elohim never revealed the purpose or true danger of the Tree of the Knowledge of Good and Evil. He put the tree there and presumably named it, but provides no justification for his prohibition of its fruit. He threatens to execute the people if they disobey. The serpent, however, provides an explanation. He assures the woman that the threat of execution will not be carried out. "You will not die *instantly*" (Gen. 3:4), he said, quoting the words of God more accurately than the woman had done.[12] "God [*elohim*] knows that when you eat of it your eyes will be opened, and you will be like God [*elohim*], knowing good and evil" (Gen. 3:5). Not only does YHWH/Elohim utter empty threats, as the serpent points out, but he also jealously guards his prerogatives, keeping the first humans in ignorance and powerlessness. The serpent accuses YHWH/Elohim of dominating the humans, holding them back in perpetual ignorance, while he and the other *elohim* enjoy supernatural knowledge and endless life. We must look hard for narrative cues suggesting how seriously we should take this accusation.

Just how accurate, then, were the serpent's predictions regarding the momentous event? YHWH/Elohim told the humans that they would die. The serpent said they would not die. Having eaten the fruit, they remained alive. The serpent said their eyes would be opened. That is exactly what happened. The serpent said that they would be like God, knowing good and evil. In contrast, when their eyes were opened, they saw that they were naked. As a result, the woman accuses the serpent of deceiving her.[13] There is a bit more to the story before we can decide whether the woman was correct. After the pronouncements of judgment, YHWH/Elohim calls a meeting of the *elohim* and makes a speech that confirms all the serpent's accusations! He says that the humans have become "like one of us, knowing good and evil" (Gen. 3:22; cf. 3:5: "You will be like *elohim*, knowing good and evil").

The serpent had accused YHWH/Elohim of deliberately

withholding divine knowledge and divine life out of human hands so as to keep them in an inferior position to himself. Now, YHWH/Elohim himself confirms the charge. He casts them out of the garden to prevent their eating from the Tree of Life, lest they "live forever" (Gen. 3:22). With the knowledge imparted by the magical tree *and* eternal life, there would be nothing to distinguish them from the *'elohim,* and that is why he drove them out.

THE CHARACTER OF YHWH/ELOHIM

I here build an analysis of Genesis 2–3 that paints YHWH/ Elohim as a monster, inexplicably opposed to the fortunes of the first humans.

YHWH/Elohim's Power Is Limited

YHWH/Elohim emerges as a divine supernatural being with significant power. He does not, however, have unlimited power nor does his power emerge unscathed from challenges to his control and supremacy. When the serpent successfully challenges his divine power, he thus demonstrates its limits and boundaries. Further, the narration limits God's power by engaging in anthropomorphism. He comes to the garden at a time of day most physically comfortable for him, when the air is moving and it is a bit cooler. He asks a number of questions, which might suggest that YHWH/Elohim does not know everything.[14] Those who believe that no fault must ever be found in the character of YHWH/Elohim must necessarily conclude that YHWH/Elohim knew the answers to the questions ("Where are you?" [Gen. 3:9]; "Who told you that you were naked?" [Gen. 3:11]; "What is this that you have done?" [Gen. 3:13]) before they were asked. Such a reader believes that if God doesn't know something, he loses his dignity.[15]

YHWH/Elohim said that if the humans ate from the Tree of Knowledge they would die. They ate, but they did not die.

Interpretation gets thick at this point. YHWH/Elohim's accuracy must, by some means, be defended. The defenses take two forms. Some claim that when the humans ate the fruit they really did die, and so the prediction came true. They died because at that moment they started to age, hurtling toward their own physical dissolution. Others claim that the moment of disobedience caused them to die spiritually; it severed their heretofore unencumbered relationship to God. However, the grammar will not easily tolerate such a reading ("on that day," "dying you shall die" [Gen. 2:17]). I doubt that anyone would ever come up with such a reading unless he were desperately searching for a way to claim that God could never be wrong.

Others claim that in fact YHWH/Elohim did not carry out his threat. He had withdrawn his intention of judgment and decided instead to show mercy, as he did when he decided to be merciful to the city of Nineveh that Jonah had placed under God's judgment.[16] This defense of God breaks down when examined in the light of the last divine speech. The concern in the speech (Gen. 3:22) seems not to be mercy or forgiveness. Rather, YHWH/Elohim seeks here to limit the damage caused by human access to the Tree of Knowledge, the damage that broke down the barrier between the 'elohim and the domain of creation. The primary, in fact the only, concern is protection of divine privilege.[17]

YHWH/Elohim's Power Expressed as Malevolence toward the Humans

A novelist, Orson Scott Card, has two characters discussing the possibility of malevolent gods:

> *Real* gods would want to teach you how to be just like them. . . . He wasn't telling her what the gods were, he was telling her what goodness was. To want other people to grow. To want other people to have all the good things

you have. And to spare them the bad things if you can. That was *goodness*.[18]

When the humans hide at the approach of YHWH/Elohim, does that point to "the fall of man," a complete corruption of their spirit because of their disobedience? There is no real indication that this is the case. Perhaps the humans were always afraid of the divine visits. The only stated difference is that now they know they are naked. It is physically apparent that they have risked divine displeasure. They hide from him, not because their souls are corrupt, but because they know that Yahweh is dangerous, or, at the very least, they are frightened. Subsequent events both within the narrative (they were interrogated and driven from the garden to a life of pain, conflict, and hardship) and immediately following this narrative (the punishment of Cain, the Flood) proved that their fears of God were well-founded.[19]

Why did YHWH/Elohim place these trees in the middle of the garden, if not to doom the humans to a terrifying failure? Why did he threaten to kill the humans if they disobeyed his commands?[20] Why did he deliberately conceal from the humans the *true* reason for his prohibition—that he did not want to share divine attributes with the humans? I come to one conclusion, and it seems inevitable: that God, for some unknown reason, sought the destruction of the humans, or at least was completely indifferent to their fate, and was concerned instead with his own comfort and position.

> If they [the gods] exist at all, they take pleasure in oppression and deception, humiliation and ignorance. They act to make other people smaller and themselves larger. These would not be gods, then, even if they existed. They would be enemies. Devils.[21]

The deity creates the initial plot conflict by placing the trees in the middle of the garden and forbidding the humans to consume their fruit. Further, the deity discovers the transgression and punishes the miscreants. YHWH/Elohim protects his realm by banishing the humans from the garden. Throughout the story YHWH/Elohim is the *problem* that the humans have to overcome.[22] YHWH/Elohim is the hindrance, the barrier that keeps the protagonists from reaching their goal: advancement, independence, and maturity.[23] YHWH/Elohim is the force against which the story and its protagonists grind and struggle. Deity in this story is like the troll that must be outwitted before one can cross the bridge, the spell that must be broken, the dragon that must be defeated, the ordeal that must be endured.

In this story, the deity plays the roles of the parents who must be left and the foe that must be vanquished. YHWH/Elohim becomes an imprisoner, seeking to keep the humans in the Garden of Eden in ignorance and dependency. The woman wanted to be wise, and the Lord of the garden denied her this. YHWH/Elohim dedicates his not inconsiderable efforts to preventing her (and her husband) from becoming wise. When they disobey and gain knowledge, he seeks to minimize their threat to his priority.

That this is a seditious notion of deity there can be no doubt. To identify this vain and petty creature with the God of ancient Israel is to create a troubling literary conflict. To what degree should other portions of the literature (whether limited to the book of Genesis or the entirety of the Hebrew Bible) determine the reading of this text? Is YHWH/Elohim to be identified with YHWH, the God of the Israelites, and to what extent? Is the serpent to be identified with Satan, or with the devil?[24] It also creates theological conflict, because we must ask whether the portrayal of God in this passage represents in any way the theological position of some faction in Israel, and what it tells us about their belief system. And carrying this line of reasoning one step further, is there any benefit to reading the narrative in this manner for contemporary, post-Holocaust understandings of deity? Might our culture be due for a resurgence of interest in a dangerous and unstable god, seeing that such a god might provide the only tenable explanation for the world as we experience it?

HISTORICAL CONSIDERATIONS

"The commonplace that the dominant classes generally produce the major texts holds also for the Hebrew Bible," according to biblical critic Roland Boer. Yet

> subversive culture also appropriates different patterns that pose a threat to their original home. . . . Interpretation then seeks to recover those other voices that have been silenced and co-opted, searching for traces and hints—normally formal—that suggest the presence of something quite different from the overt messages of the text.[25]

Boer notes that certain positions are submerged within the text, and these might not represent the majority position. One might discover them through an examination of the formal structural conflicts within the narrative. The seditious story I have read from Genesis 2–3 is just one of the stories that incompletely inhabit the space of this text. There is also a traditional story that struggles with the monstrous reading. Each reading contains a key element that undermines its credibility and points to the opposite interpretation. If God is monstrous, why does he cover the first humans with animal skins after he drives them from the garden? Such an activity bespeaks tender concern and nurturing, exactly the behavior we don't expect from a monster.[26] We see in such behavior benevolent concern, rather than malevolent hatred or incomprehensibility. There is no way to incorporate this incident into the reading I propose. Likewise, if we examine what I call the theological reading[27] of the Genesis story, in which God is good, having all knowledge and all power, we get stuck on YHWH/Elohim's threat to

execute the couple, which was never carried out. This under-
cuts the authority of the theological reading.

So when I consider the historical underpinnings of the Genesis 2–3 narrative, I expect to receive at least two sets of answers. Because the text is a site of conflict, no one reading
completely dominates the other. Of course, there is usually a
master reading, the one that seems to support the views of
those who control the institutions of power in Israel. This reading sees the story from the perspective of the authority of the
Israelite God. The narrative exhorts the hearers/readers to
obey diligently the commandments of God and be wary of the
consequences of disobedience.

When the story is examined from the perspective of a dangerous god, however, a dramatically different pattern begins to
emerge. The woman and the man, by means of necessary trans-
formation, attain new levels of independence, responsibility,
and maturity. They achieve this by going through ordeal and
test. YHWH/Elohim, the evil authority figure, resists their
growth. What group in Israel might represent its ideas through
such a story? Anarchists? Revolutionaries? Some organized
protest movement among the sages? Atheists and cynics? It is
impossible to say, but clearly some seditious group or individual has entered the most sacred fields of canonical literature
and planted seeds of dissent.

The structure of the story is seditious because it is a movement from transgression to punishment and at the same time
a movement from infancy to adulthood (or at least adoles-
cence), from naïveté to maturity, from innocence to knowledge. A Freudian reading suggests that one must inevitably
break with the "Father" in order to become a full, mature human. The Fall is a necessary fall, or perhaps not a fall at all but
rather a graduation.

The character of God is seditious, particularly when placed
within the book of Genesis, whose editors were radical monothe-

ists. This God demonstrates the character flaws of insecurity and jealousy. A clever serpent that he himself had made can outsmart him, and his humans thwart his commands. He blusters in anger against the humans because of his own fear of competition. This is not a flattering portrayal. To undermine the character of a nation's chief or only deity is to undermine all the nation's institutions of authority that are thought to have been granted by divine sanction. For example, virtually every king in Israel and Judah felt it necessary to demonstrate that his authority derived from YHWH, whether through charismatic choice (Saul, David, Jeroboam) or through divine succession (Solomon, Rehoboam, the Davidic line). So to undermine the authority of the Israelite God was to undermine the Israelite system of government. This was true to an even greater extent during the postexilic period when the Temple priesthood wielded great power, and government was inextricably linked to a particular theological position.

YHWH/Elohim opposes the humans and seeks their destruction for no apparent reason. God manifests himself to the humans as a monster. The question that disturbs me, haunts me, is, What sort of historical class or interest group portrays its own god as a monster? Texts such as this one notoriously resist efforts to locate them precisely in the reconstructed history of Israel. Does this story originate in early monarchy, or among the inhabitants of the Second Temple period? Perhaps an examination of the implications of this monstrous god might bring things more into focus.

A traditional rendering of God supports the entrenched structures of ancient Israelite society. In such a rendering, the narrative supports the authority of YHWH/Elohim invariably at every turn. Likewise, the truthfulness and reliability of the *words* of YHWH/Elohim are defended. God knows that they will disobey; God knows where they are when they hide from him; God knew who told them they were naked and whether or not they had eaten from the tree he had forbidden.

There is no limit to God's power, no limit even to his power over the serpent.

A traditional rendering would regard the judgments of YHWH/Elohim against the serpent, the woman, and the man as righteous and appropriate, regarding the transgressions of the humans as heinous. The deity cannot be incorrect in any of his statements, and therefore if YHWH/Elohim said that the humans would die on that day, then in some way that we have difficulty understanding, they certainly *did* die. The story supports the *rules* that produce order and control within the society. The origin stories, the etiologies, serve to confirm the status quo. There are good reasons, such a story claims, that things are the way they are, and they *should not change.*

Elements within the Garden of Eden story reverse this rendering and declare that the authority of God must be questioned.[28] This was a hidden but not-so-subtle questioning of the structures and authorities in Israelite society. God is a monster, and his designated representatives, whether the palace bureaucracy of King David's court or the hierocracy of the Persian period, are monstrous too.

I suspect, however, that there is more here than just a negation, "This is the God I do not serve." There is also the sense of the assertion "If there is a god then she/he must be monstrous. How else can we make sense of such a horrible world, except to posit a horrible God?"

CONCLUSION

Graham Greene, in *The Honorary Consul,* deals with this question:

> Free will was the excuse for everything. It was God's alibi. They had never read Freud. Evil was made by man or Satan. It was simple that way. But I could never believe in Satan. It was much easier to believe that God was evil. . . .

> I believe in the evil of God . . . but I believe in His goodness
> too. . . . But I see no other way to believe in God. The God
> I believe in must be responsible for all the evil as well as
> for all the Saints. . . . It is a big struggle and a long suffer-
> ing evolution, and I believe God is suffering the same evo-
> lution that we are, but perhaps with more pain.[29]

There is always something terribly hopeful in such nega-
tions, such denials of the goodness of God. Those in power frequently impose notions of God's goodness upon the backs of
those who suffer privation. A negation of the God embodied in
theological language is also a rejection of the craven desires of
earthly despots. It undermines the notion of a good, all-
powerful God, a notion that cannot be reconciled with all the
pain in the world. It affirms the marginalized classes, which
might include the Canaanites, the poor, or women. It exposes
the justifications and mystifications of the ruling classes.

When might such seditious ideas have gained currency with
the Israelite community? We have no effective way to determine this. Imaginatively, a number of reconstructions are possible. The opposition indicated by the presence of such a
conflicted text, a seditious formulation of deity, might be gen-
erational (old against young); economic (rich against poor);
geographic (north against south or urban against agricultural);
religious (Baalists against Yahwists). In any of these or a host
of possible others, we might identify the excesses of
YHWH/Elohim with the excesses of the leaders of the dominant group. Or perhaps it is a negative theological attack on
Yahwism because of personal or national despair, offering
nothing in exchange, making the claim that Yahwism doesn't
work. There is insufficient information, however, to ground
these observations in a particular time, place, or author.

The text is hopeful because it empowers individuals to say
no to injustice in high places. It is also hopeful because it

suggests the possibility that there might be gods (or understandings of God) who cannot be linked with the structural in-
equities of society.

> After the final no there comes a yes
> And on that yes the future world depends,
> No was the night.
>
> Wallace Stevens,
> "The Well-Dressed Man with a Beard"

Uzzah, YHWH's Friend:
The *Irrational* God
(2 Samuel 6)

People sometimes talk of God's love as if it's a pleasant thing.
But it is terrible in a way. Think of all it includes . . . But surely
God's love includes people who can't bear it.

Wendell Berry, Fidelity: Five Stories

THE FIRST STORY

I have lost two sons to that damn ark, may I be forgiven for saying it. And I am not the only one. Father Aaron, leader of our clan, lost two of his sons as well. Nadab and Abihu died before the LORD, but we all know it was the ark that killed them.

My first son, Eleazar, died while serving the ark in my house.[1] My second son, Uzzah, died accompanying the ark to Jerusalem. Both sons died too young and mysteriously. A father should never live to see his sons die. Uzzah and his brother Ahio accompanied the ark when David decided to bring it to Jerusalem. We placed it on a new oxcart. For whatever reason, the oxen stumbled. The story, as I heard it, gets muddled here. Was the ark about to tip over? It appears so.

And my son Uzzah, bless his memory, reached out to steady the sacred box, YHWH's throne. There is absolutely no truth to the rumors that he grabbed it with disrespect, with contempt. Why would he do that, he who along with his other brothers was raised in the presence of the ark and taught by me to show it appropriate respect . . . and fear? And just like that, he was lying there, dead, without warning. Scared David. He didn't know whether to be angry that YHWH spoiled his parade, or afraid he would follow Uzzah to the grave. And he placed as much distance between himself and the ark as he could manage.

Uzzah always seemed unfairly put upon. After all, he was just trying to steady the ark, to keep it from falling into the mud. What could be wrong in that? Killed for being a conscientious person, Uzzah emerges as a sympathetic figure in the story. But if Uzzah is sympathetic, the Israelite God is irrational. My analysis of 2 Samuel 6, the story of Uzzah, examines some early explanations for the death of Uzzah, and what it might mean for people who tell such stories about their God.

This event occurs in a busy chapter, one in which David dances suggestively in the company of his lowliest servants, and in which he and Michal openly vent their hostility toward each other. In this chapter David brings the ark to Jerusalem, his city, and gains control over the institutions of Israel.[2] And yet, humble Uzzah, who only wanted to protect the ark from profanation, or defilement, is struck dead, and his death colors all these other events.[3] Two different narratives emerge from the reading of 2 Samuel 6 itself, and another from its retelling by the Chronicler.

I think an ancient narrator, the writer of the biblical account, would expect readers to picture Uzzah as suddenly, in the performance of his duties, keeling over dead. This is not one of those stories in which YHWH appears in human form, eats a meal, and has his feet washed. Nor is this an account of lightning bolts from the altar, or from heaven, or the earth swallowing someone up. The people inferred divine wrath from the sudden and unexplained death of Uzzah. Evidence for this includes the fact that there is no mention of YHWH as a physical presence, no description of the manner of death.

The presence of the ark serves as the manifestation of YHWH in the passage.

GAPS IN THE TEXT

At every crucial interpretive crux, this passage breaks down into near-insoluble problems. The object of the verb "reach out" is missing in verse 6. The Chronicler (1 Chron. 13:9) supplies it: "When they came to the threshing floor of Chidon, Uzzah *put out his hand to hold the ark,* for the oxen shook it" (emphasis added). The Chronicler added "his hand" as the thing that Uzzah "reached out." Most subsequent interpreters follow this lead. In another example of the breakdown of meaning, we note that YHWH struck the young priest because of Uzzah's *hashal* or *hasal.* This Hebrew word provides many problems for the translator. It occurs only here, with a weak connection to similar sounding words in cognate languages,[4] and almost always is understood according to the translator's understanding of the context in this passage. So, in order to provide a meaning for this word, one must already have decided what Uzzah has done. To use some general word, such as "transgression," would seem most prudent at this point.[5] The verse would then read "YHWH struck him there because of his transgression."

We cannot determine exactly what the oxen did that precipitated these events. The lexicographical information just is not available. We *assume* they stumbled. The verb means "to let drop" [something] and requires an object. We *assume* that when they stumbled, they dislodged the ark, although the story never says this. We *assume* that the ark was about to fall, and then we *assume* that Uzzah stretched out his hand. Not a single one of these assumptions resides in the actual words on the page.[6] They all represent reconstructive efforts to tame and make sense of a difficult text.

So the "story" we tell from this "text" is almost completely imaginary, but that doesn't render such interpretations worthless. When we speak of 2 Samuel 6:6–10, the story of Uzzah, we are not speaking of the text itself (the words on the page) but rather a reader's imaginative projection upon that text. Still, in the different "readings" (for lack of a better word) of Uzzah that follow, there is much of the person/persons who fashioned it, whether the Deuteronomist or the Chronicler or some other early storyteller.

WHAT UZZAH DID

I offer three explanations as to why Uzzah died. The first one focuses only on the details within the text of 2 Samuel 6:6–10 itself. Reading 2 Samuel along with 1 Chronicles 13 provides an alternative source of meaning, rendering it a different story. Both of these stories seek to justify the action of God against Uzzah. They make Uzzah's death somehow understandable and even fair. The first accomplishes this by emphasizing the seriousness of Uzzah's crime; the second, by drawing attention away from Uzzah (a sympathetic character) and toward the issue of a larger technical cultic disagreement. David, who exists on the fringe of the other two stories, probably added by a later editor, develops a third explanation that I will examine afterward.

Uzzah Faces the Irrational God

Uzzah did such a terrible thing that he deserved to die. In order to understand this assertion, it becomes necessary to discuss in more depth the meaning of the ark. The statement, "Uzzah reached out his hand to the ark . . . and took hold of it. . . . God struck [Uzzah] there . . . and he died . . . " nearly equals "YHWH killed Uzzah because he touched the ark."[7] Touching the ark offends because it means the same thing as touching YHWH.

At the point where 2 Samuel 6 mentions the ark, YHWH floods into the narrative. Uzzah died "beside the ark of God," which I take to mean "in God's presence," an idea often communicated by the Hebrew phrase "before the LORD."[8] In many places where the text says "before the LORD," it appears to refer to actions that the Israelites ritually performed in front of the ark.[9] When David finally brought the ark into his city, its entrance is treated as if YHWH himself walked through Jerusalem's gates. The ceremony has that exalted sense, as illustrated by the psalm often associated with this event: "Lift up your heads, O gates! and be lifted up, O ancient doors! that the King of glory may come in. Who is the King of glory? . . . YHWH of hosts, he is the King of Glory" (Ps. 24:7–10).[10] When David dances before the ark, he dances *before YHWH,* as he insists to his wife Michal. "It was *before the* LORD [emphasis added], who chose me . . . [and] I will make merry *before the* LORD" (2 Sam. 6:21).[11]

That is why touching the ark might have seemed so heinous to the ancient readers of this story. When Uzzah touched the ark, grasping it, he was grasping God, and such an action was both forward and inappropriate, showing disrespect and presumed power over YHWH. YHWH struck Uzzah to punish him for his show of disrespect. Uzzah just stumbled upon a place where YHWH's power lay unshielded, unprotected by sanctioned ritual, and was struck dead automatically, electrocuted, so to speak.

In 2 Samuel 6 the ark *means YHWH.*[12] Therefore, when Uzzah touches the ark inappropriately, he dies. However, the ark has the opposite effect upon the household of Obed-edom, the ark's next repository. YHWH blesses this family because YHWH (the ark) is a guest within their house. Therefore we may conclude that in the case of Uzzah and in the case of Obed-edom the ark represents YHWH's presence.

Israel's Careless Priests

Again defending Uzzah's punishment as appropriate, the second version of this story, which is given by the Chronicler, sees Uzzah's death as God's legitimate reaction to the profanation of the ark, although it points to a different profanation entirely. Uzzah lies dead, the Chronicler writes, because Uzzah and his brother had used an improper conveyance to deliver the ark from the house of Abinadab to Jerusalem. "Because you did not carry it the first time, the LORD our God burst out against us, because we did not give it proper care" (1 Chron. 15:12–13). We can find some evidence for this explanation in the original story, in 2 Samuel 6. There we read that the Israelites carried the ark from Abinadab's house in an oxcart. But when the ark left the house of Obed-edom, the priests[13] carried the ark on their shoulders. Although many other things changed between the two processions,[14] from this one change the Chronicler concludes that the transgression for which YHWH punished Uzzah was the oxcart itself. The Chronicler believed that when they carried the ark in the correct manner, YHWH would not get angry with them and they would be safe.

This reading supports the interests of a Jerusalem-based priesthood.[15] For the first time it links the ark, a northern, non-monarchic tradition, with Jerusalem in the south. This way of reading the story demonstrates the incompetence of a particular non-Jerusalemite priesthood (and by extension, all non-Jerusalemite priesthoods) and the expertise of the priests who carried the ark into Jerusalem.[16] At the time that Samuel was written however, no one cared how the ark must be carried. As early as the time of Solomon, no one moved it around any longer. Perhaps the storyteller desired to elevate a particular guild of the priesthood (the Jerusalemite) by associating it positively with the ark. It is the means by which that group appropriates the priestly traditions of another. There is some hint of this preference of one group of priests over another with regard to the ark in Numbers 4:

When the camp is to set out, Aaron and his sons shall go in and take down the screening curtain, and cover the ark of the covenant with it . . . and shall put its poles in place" (vv. 5–6). [The Kohathites] must not touch the holy things, or they will die (v. 15). But the Kohathites must not go in to look on the holy things even for a moment; otherwise they will die (v. 20).[17]

David handed over the ark to a different guild of priests, a guild that did not convey the god on a sacred cart (as the Philistines did), but rather on their own backs.[18]

So the Chronicler's interpretation of 2 Samuel 6 portrays the oxcart as an act of rebellion against a holy god. Anyone familiar with the law in Numbers 4:15 should know that only priests must carry the ark. This oversight resulted from the ignorance of the priestly "impersonators" (Uzzah and his brother). David corrected this by bringing in the experts, the ones who knew the proper manner to handle such palpable holiness.

So, to recap, I have explored two interpretations of the Uzzah story. In the first, based on information provided only in 2 Samuel, YHWH is angry with Uzzah for inappropriately touching his ark, which he (YHWH) identifies with his own divine person. In the second, the unqualified and probably illegitimate priests, Uzzah and his brother, brought down YHWH's anger because they carried the ark in an oxcart, instead of on their shoulders as was proper. Then the ark was given to the appropriate authorities, the Jerusalem priests.[19]

It is difficult to determine the origin of the first story. It seems early, primitive, simplistic. The God of this story is very primal. God is still unquestionable, and so by extension, his representatives would be. But which representatives? An earlier group of priests? The royal house of David? Or might we find the origin even further back in some ur-story, in support of a village elder? David, however, hovering at the edge of this story, offers us a third possibility, one I find intriguing, to say the least.

David Repudiates Divine Irrationality

"David was angry because the LORD had burst forth with an outburst upon Uzzah. . . . David was afraid of the LORD that day"[20] (2 Sam. 6:8–9). While David's emotions swing from anger, to fear, to relief, his first reaction to Uzzah's death, anger, seems most revealing. Fear is the conventional, the appropriate, response to divine wrath. But only rarely do we glimpse an individual venting anger against YHWH and against divine judgment.[21] One can only speculate *why* David lashed out against YHWH. Perhaps Uzzah's death offended David's sense of the orderliness of the universe, the predictability of events. Perhaps YHWH had offended David's sense of justice—it was simply unfair of YHWH to demand that Uzzah should have known not to touch the ark. David believed that YHWH killed Uzzah for no good reason. Perhaps David was angry at the waste of a good, young life for the sake of trivialities. Or else, David's anger was because YHWH put an end to his parade. His anger would then be that of a spoiled child.

In any case, fear quickly replaced the anger. David realized that YHWH threatened not merely his parade but his very existence! "How can the ark of God come into my care?" (lit., "come unto me"), David asked. At that point, David distanced himself from the ark, and from YHWH, leaving it in the household of Obed-edom. David regarded YHWH and the ark as dangerous, liable to break out against him at any moment.

David regarded the ark as a manifestation of YHWH, if not YHWH himself. Further, David believed that YHWH *ought not* to have killed Uzzah. David strongly disapproved of YHWH's action. He did not direct his anger against priests who perhaps by cultic error had made God angry. He directed his anger against YHWH, who unnecessarily and unfairly murdered someone who worked for him. However, his anger turned to fear when he realized that YHWH might just as easily murder him.[22]

He regarded the very presence of the ark as a threat; he removed it to a house not only outside the gates of his city, but, if Obed-edom is a non-Israelite, outside the nation of Israel itself, banishing it to the unknown realm of the other.

If one believes that YHWH ought not to have done this to Uzzah, that means that Uzzah did nothing wrong to merit his death. Uzzah was an innocent. Uzzah's innocent behavior did not save him from divine destruction. He was still at risk from a violent, unpredictable God. YHWH killed him not because he touched the ark, nor because he carried it in an oxcart, but only because Uzzah found himself in the wrong place at the wrong time, a time when YHWH was in a terrible mood.

CONCLUSION

Why did Uzzah die? Three distinct answers to that question emerge: (1) YHWH struck Uzzah because he touched the ark; (2) in the Chronicler's reading of the story, Uzzah's death was a result of carrying the ark in an oxcart; (3) in a kind of epilogue, another character, David, reacts to Uzzah's death after the event; he rejects the God who caused it, redirecting the anger back to YHWH.

Both the Chronicler's reading and the reading through the eyes of David's character are "back readings," that is, efforts to change or transform the meaning of a previously existing text.[23] The Chronicler makes God petty; David makes God a dangerous, unpredictable force that can break out against anyone at any moment. Why would the Israelites tell such stories about their God? To regard God as violent contrasts with the more common understanding of God as pleasant, benevolent, and all wise. This belief in a mad god or a chaos-god, which occurs in the story of Uzzah, brings me to make the three observations that follow.

1. This story *reflects* the Israelites' experience. These were a people who believed that God was the underlying cause for all things that happened, especially disease, accident, conquest— the big things. Many therefore imagined their God as an exacting judge who expected far more than his people could ever deliver, so God was perpetually angry with them and justified in punishing them. Whenever something bad happened, it should be interpreted as God punishing them for their sins. This approach resembles that of the royal narratives of Samuel and Kings, and it is the argument of Job's friends. But there are also those, like David, who believe that God's punishment was not always just. As in the case of Uzzah, they affirm that God is frequently irrational and cannot be trusted. That is the way they experienced reality.

2. In addition to this first observation (that such stories reflect the experience of people trying to make sense of bewildering suffering), this story also prescribes an appropriate *response* to such suffering. It counsels us not to accept evil quietly, stoically, but to lash out in anger, like David, against the God who has brought on this suffering. And according to this reckoning, one must maintain this anger, not as a passing stage, moving toward passive acceptance, but rather as an appropriate, holy response, one which rejects the divine being.

3. Finally, this construction of God (such as we may find in the story of Uzzah) troubles the sure notions many in Israel had as to what God was like. It surrounds God in appropriate mystery and confusion. We cannot accept the notion of a god who would slay Uzzah for such a minor indiscretion. Might it be possible to approach the mystery of Uzzah's death from some different perspective on the divine being? Such a different perspective is not present within the text we have, but with our minds and imagination (and the inspiration of the Holy Spirit) might we not construct a god more congruent with our own ethical standards? Or must we despair of ever understanding

the death of innocents, or comprehending the God who might or might not be behind such deaths?

The ark had moved from the house of Abinadab, probably a family of Israelite priests, to the house of Obed-edom, described as an inhabitant from Gath, a Philistine city. The ark stayed with Abinadab for many years, but caused the death of Abinadab's son. It stayed with Obed-edom three months, and (we are told) YHWH blessed his household. In conclusion, I would like to offer the story from his perspective, as I would imagine it.

THE SECOND STORY

He and David went way back. Obed-edom served as one of David's mighty men. He was not the only Philistine that had joined David's band when David lived on the borderlands, but he was the only one who continued to worship the Philistine pantheon. That was not the way to get ahead in David's palace bureaucracy. David was riding his popularity on the crest of a religious outburst partly of his own making.

When Obed-edom had his fill of fighting, he retired with his family to a country estate, on the road between Kiriath-Jearim and Jerusalem. Mostly he remained undisturbed, tending his fields and his household, which by this time had grown substantial.

When YHWH struck Uzzah dead on the threshing floor of Nacon, David was angry and frightened. The sacred object that David had believed would tighten his hold over the nation now proved to be a liability. Should he send it back to Abinadab, from whence it had come? Too far—he didn't want to be responsible for it any longer than necessary. His old friend Obed-edom lived somewhere around here. Leave it with him. Isn't there some priestcraft in his background? He did not serve YHWH, but at least he'd have some idea what to do. And the death of a non-Israelite wouldn't affect the king's popularity the way Uzzah's death had.

So they brought the ark to the estate of Obed-edom, who had very mixed feelings about the matter. He knew how important this object was to the Israelites, and to David, and he could see how upset David was—he had never seen him so afraid. And he wondered for the safety of his family. He knew how many people had mysteriously died when they contacted the ark in some way, both Israel's friends and its enemies. But what could he say?

He would keep it in the front storage room. The servants would clear out the room, give it a fresh coat of bright blue and red paint (he had never lost his Philistine affection for bright colors in this washed-out land). Erect an altar of incense and place an oil lamp, and they would be set. That was all this Israelite god might reasonably expect of him. He certainly wasn't going to slaughter animals on its behalf.

It was done as he commanded. A servant was to keep the oil lamp filled and lit, and Obed-edom himself would come down every morning and evening and prepare and burn the incense. He found himself lingering after the ceremony.

He rejoiced when his son and daughter-in-law announced her first pregnancy after many years of trying. He had despaired of grandchildren. When two long-standing debtors paid off their account that same week he was amused, thinking strange thoughts. When a close relative died and he inherited a huge tract of land, and another piece of property he had wanted to buy for years came on the market for much less than its value, he got a little afraid. But finally, when his wife announced her own pregnancy, word spread throughout the community that YHWH had blessed this Gittite because of the ark of God. Obed-edom supposed that this was so.

When word came to David how YHWH had blessed his old comrade, the king rushed down to Obed-edom's house and took the ark away. The servants awoke their master early one morning. The king, hundreds of troops, wailing livestock, and a whole retinue of priests waited outside his gate. What could Obed-edom say? He directed the priests to the storeroom. The priests clicked their tongues and made signs of disapproval and warding off when they saw the arrangements he had made for the ark. After a brief conference with the king, the appointed priests carried out the ark on the poles they had brought, and set it before a stone altar that Moabite slaves were rapidly constructing. When the company made ready to leave, they slaughtered their animals on the altar and burned them entire. Obed-edom had never seen the king so intimidated, standing before the ark sweating as he waited the outcome of the sacrifice. When he saw approval on the faces of the priests he let out a long sigh of relief. The crowd was infected with David's changed mood, and the whole party began rejoicing as they marched down the road with the ark.

Obed-edom never allowed the servants to put the grain jars and jars of wine back in that front storeroom. He kept up the altar of incense and oil lamp. He sat in that room often, staring at the empty space where the ark used to be.

He never had a streak of good luck such as the time the ark was in his house, but Obed-edom lived a long and happy life, and his children maintained the altar and oil lamp after his death as a family shrine. But many years later his oldest son placed an image in the room, because he could never understand why their father rendered honor in the direction of a place where nothing was.

The Fatal Census:
The *Vindictive* God
(2 Samuel 24)

. . . the gods themselves are not forever glad. The ineffaceable, sad birthmark in the brow of man is but the stamp of sorrow in the signers.

Herman Melville, Moby Dick

A simple description of the events in this census narrative in 2 Samuel always astounds me. It is the most Kafkaesque passage in the entire Bible. As in *The Trial*, we have an accused criminal who seems more the victim of the fancy of some higher power than the actual perpetrator of a crime. So in 2 Samuel 24 David appears to be a hapless victim. Perhaps, as in Kafka's strange novel, we sympathize and identify with the bewilderment of the protagonist, who has lost confidence in a fair universe.

We are told in the introduction to the passage that YHWH is angry with Israel and seeks an occasion to punish them. "Again the anger of the LORD was kindled against Israel" (2 Sam. 24:1a). There is no literary context to this pronouncement.[1] We know nothing of what might be the cause of YHWH's anger: Was it anything that Israel had done? Was it their fault, or completely unexpected? Because there is no trace of a notion of a cause on Israel's part—that is, there is nothing mentioned that Israel had done—one is inclined to assume that this blast of YHWH's anger was uncaused, as impersonal as solar flares that blast forth from the sun.

The import of the next verses dramatically changes because of this introduction. If we took out the first verse, the narrative would appear as a straightforward appeal to avoid displeasing a deity by not doing proscribed behavior.[2] David and Israel were punished because he (David) commanded a census, which is a proscribed behavior. But when the narrative is framed by the pronouncement that this is *caused* by YHWH's anger, everything that follows is skewed somehow. Now we know and will expect that whatever follows is the means by which YHWH will afflict Israel.

THE ANGER OF YHWH AGAINST ISRAEL

Two things must be considered immediately. Why is a census regarded as a horrifying action fraught with spiritual consequences? And, since YHWH causes this evil census, how do we deal with the possibility of God tempting people to evil?

The Census: State-Sponsored Immorality

Regarding the immorality issue, it is possible that negative overtones to the notion of census taking were familiar to the audience of 2 Samuel and its antecedents. But is it possible to reconstruct the reason for the prohibition? A census is always taken for a reason, never just out of idle curiosity. States count citizens in order to assess their military strength or determine the strength of their resources. David's sin might be his lack of faith in YHWH's ability to provide, his compulsion to find out for himself if he had the military and civilian resources to expand his territory.

Although such concerns might have played a factor in the negative reaction to the census, the more significant reason has to do with the power that the census knowledge gives, power that enables governments to take those resources when they need them, without regard to the personal freedom of individual families. The rabbis, however, marveled at David's stupidity, that he did not know what every school child knows,[3] that one must make atonement for every young man counted in Israel. In Exodus 30:11–16, YHWH enjoins Moses *when* he takes a census to make sure that each person counted must pay half a shekel, a "ransom for their lives" (v. 12). As attractive as such a theory might be, there are problems with it. First, there is no hint in 1 Samuel of David's oversight. Second, the anger of YHWH comes *before* David takes the census, not afterward. A failure to sacrifice cannot account for YHWH's desire to see Israelites die.

A census was a license to tax and to conscript. This act struck Joab, David's commander, as a horrid violation of social polity, and he implored David to forego his determination to take a census. "May the LORD your God increase the number of the people a hundredfold, while the eyes of my lord the king can still see it! But why does my lord the king want to do this" (2 Sam. 24:3)? The strong language of Joab to his sovereign barely avoids transgressing the proper, public respect that he owes David. But in the end Joab must obey the explicit directions. After the completion of the census, David himself, realizing the magnitude of what he had just done, reacts with horror and self-loathing, "I have sinned greatly in what I have done. But now, O LORD, I pray you, take away the guilt of your servant; for I have done very foolishly" (2 Sam. 24:10). It appears, as much as we can determine, that the "crime" of the census is David's violation of the ancient tribal structure of Israel. Instead of individual tribes who mobilized their citizenry in the face of national threat, now the centralized government, newly informed of its resources by means of the census, would be able to command its citizens to assemble.

God Commands Sin

The second concern regards the possibility of deity tempting anyone to evil. Once we have established that (1) God initiated the census, and (2) that the census was a grave violation of some aspects of Israel's code, a serious theological problem asserts itself. In a world of many gods, the notion of evil gods, or gods who work against the divine moral order, or even mischievous gods, is not inconceivable. However, a nation commanded to worship only one God must be able to regard that God as reliably good.

But a totally good god cannot account for the presence of evil in the world. So the various biblical materials work hard either to absolve God from wrongdoing, or more expansively, to portray a god responsible for all things, good and evil. In our time, a distinction is often made between *moral* evil and *natural* evil in the Hebrew Bible. The ancient texts appear to make no such distinction. For example, I am struck with second Isaiah's solemn pronouncement, "I form light and create darkness, I make weal and create woe; I YHWH do all these things" (Isa. 45:7).[4] At least some in Israel drew some significant inferences about their refusal to worship other gods—that YHWH would be held responsible for everything.

So in this passage, 2 Samuel 24, God compels and deceives humans to do something wicked. The Hebrew word *tsavah*, command, is possibly left out of the passage by design. The word used here is *sut*, usually translated "enticed." This word frequently involves some notion of tricking somebody into doing something. It is unusual to associate *sut* with deity.[5] "Commandment," most frequently associated by Jews with the Halakah, the requirements of God found in the Torah, is reserved for those special sacred requirements. *Sut* suggests the demonic, the bad side, and puts YHWH's "requirements" here in a different light. Perhaps they should be resisted, and David's culpability is that he took a census against his own better judgment, out of loyalty to YHWH. He should have put his foot down!

But, as has been mentioned earlier, the narrator does not

directly address this issue. The tension we feel over the passage stems from the theological categories we ourselves bring to it. It is impossible to say whether or not the narrator had a difficult time with the concept of God requiring a wicked thing. Does this divine act reflect a general theological attitude held by society at that time, or was the narrator deliberately baiting the readers by accepting easily something that would appear to others as horrifying? Until the time of the Holocaust, such notions were infrequently examined in the Jewish, the Christian, or the scholarly traditions. When discussed at all among scholars, such notions (of a dangerous, unpredictable god) were consigned to the earliest "pagan" roots of Israel, long ago forsaken by the subsequent enlightened Israelite communities.

What we can be sure of is that every succeeding generation feels a tension between what they *want* to think about God and the behavior of the God who participates in this narrative. Interestingly, this story is placed at the very end of 2 Samuel, with no transitions that connect it to any other narrative.[6] How embarrassing this passage must have been to subsequent tradents.

In the book of Job, YHWH afflicts the protagonist who had been declared innocent in the prologue, once by the narrator and twice by God. Job's vivid description of being ruthlessly pursued by an irrationally angry deity stays uneasily in the mind. The thorns, the arrows, and the ravening teeth tearing at Job create tension with the consistently benevolent deity found in most of the psalms or much of Samuel-Kings. In Job, as in 2 Samuel 24, God is untrustworthy.

In the Christian testament we have a similar struggle between the notion that God is responsible for all the things that happen, even the bad things, and the notion that God is responsible only for the good. The Lord's Prayer encourages us to plead with God not to entice us toward temptation (Matt. 6:13, Luke 11:4), while James contends to the contrary, "No one, when tempted, should say 'I am tempted by God'; for God cannot be tempted by evil, and he himself tempts no one" (James 1:13). The same conflict existed during the entirety of Israelite history. In 2 Samuel 24 we have clear indication that for God's own intentions, the Divine *will* on occasion push someone in the direction of sinful behavior.

And in this case God had a purpose—seeking occasion against Israel, an excuse to punish the people. So if YHWH can trick Israel into doing something really bad, then YHWH would be able to punish Israel in good conscience.[7] In another example of this behavior, the rabbis speak indirectly of God's child abuse. They tell the story of

> a man who struck his son a strong blow, and then put a plaster on his wound, saying to him, "My son! As long as this plaster is on your wound you can eat and drink at will, and bathe in hot or cold water, without fear. But if you remove it, it will break out into sores." Even so did the Blessed Holy One speak unto Israel: "My children! I created the Evil Impulse, but I [also] created the Torah, as its antidote; if you occupy yourselves with the Torah, you will not be delivered into its [the evil impulse's] hand."[8]

So God both wounds and heals. Is the healing so dramatically wonderful that it is worth the initial wounding? I doubt it.

So YHWH wants to punish Israel and is willing to use his divine authority to compel Israel to sin. The word "sin" clearly would not refer to the modern notions of sin and the responsibility that it imposes on human behavior. Many contemporary ethical formulations claim that unless the sinning subject consciously chooses sinful behavior, such an individual is not culpable. In fact, such an act does not qualify as sin at all. Contrary to this, a dominant Israelite view, characteristically early but not exclusively so, states that any violation of code, even if (as in the census) only an implied violation, constitutes a sin, even in the rare occasion when the given violation was done at the behest of YHWH.

Sin is primarily understood here as transgression of cultic boundaries, but those boundaries shift through time. When Saul sees fit to offer sacrifice to YHWH, Samuel condemns him roundly, for Saul has "not kept the commandment of the LORD your God, which he commanded you" (1 Sam. 13:13). Although no place in the written material is there a prohibition of kingly sacrifice,[9] Saul accepts the condemnation as justified and valid. But some years later, when David offers sacrifice to enable the entrance of the ark into Jerusalem (2 Samuel 6), no one condemns him for cultic infraction. And even though his wife, Saul's daughter, castigates David's lack of kingly dignity, she doesn't refer to her father's sacrifice and Samuel's condemnation of that activity.

I make two points from this reference to other royal stories in 1 Samuel: (1) there existed in the Israelite literature this category of unspecified or unexpected cultic infraction, and they regarded such infractions seriously; and (2) these transgressions might tend to shift in importance through the passage of time. However, when these rules are in force, they are always regarded as self-evident, permanently binding, and a terrible transgression. Thus, although a census can seem so horrible to them, it appears innocuous to us.

Cultic infraction in "savage" societies leaves little room for one to hide behind technicalities. Therefore, David could not argue, "Well, I knew a census was wrong, but I thought for this higher good of Israel's military security, I could do it just this one time."[10] Nor could David claim, "My intentions were good." It didn't matter whether or not his intentions were good. All that mattered was that he did the act. The action itself, independent of motivation, brings condemnation. Therefore, YHWH justly punished Israel, even though YHWH was ultimately the one responsible for the sinful act.

1 Chronicles—A Sanitized Version of the Story

It becomes relatively easy for a later editor, embarrassed by YHWH's behavior in the earlier passage, to erase these earlier references to YHWH and replace them with the Hebrew word customarily translated "Satan."[11] The simple substitution of one word, "YHWH," with another, "Satan," transforms the entire passage, even though most of the rest of the account is identical, nearly word-for-word.[12] The passage in 1 Chronicles 21 produces a *completely different* meaning. The problem here is that David listened to the wrong supernatural voice, Satan's, one that turned him away from the loyalty that YHWH required.[13]

The Chronicler made this change for deliberate, carefully conceived theological reasons. This writer wanted to exonerate God from any complicity in Israel's sinful behavior. The Chronicler's God is perfectly righteous or, as the writer of 1 John states, "God is light and in him there is no darkness at all" (1 John 1:5). The notion of an all encompassing, though sinning, God was not at all useful to the Chronicler.

DAVID FACES THE VINDICTIVE GOD

His Heart Strikes Him

After the census, David's "heart" struck him. He responded by saying: "I have sinned greatly in what I have done. But now, O LORD, I pray you, take away the guilt of your servant; for I have done very foolishly" (2 Sam. 24:10). One thing that surprises me in David's reaction is that he never seems struck with the injustice of his position. He never says, "But you told me to do it, God!" Why does he not? Such questioning would certainly be consistent with other literary portrayals of David, either as he is represented in the "histories" of 1 and 2 Samuel, or as the putative author of many psalms. This literary David frequently asks God "Why?" But here, in this passage, he doesn't. Why not?

One might argue that David is subtly protesting the unfairness of what he was enticed to do. It could be that the question is somehow implied though not spoken in what David actually does say—that the strong language that he uses regarding the "sin/foolish act" in fact castigates YHWH as much as, if not more than, David. If a census was a wicked/foolish act, it was wicked and foolish for God to ask for one. David's comment is something akin to Adam's defense against YHWH's accusations, "the woman whom *you* gave to be with me, she gave me fruit from the tree, and I ate" (Gen. 3:12, emphasis added). It is almost as if one is saying thus to God, "It's your fault, YHWH, that I've sinned." In fact, in these stories it *is* God's fault. But I don't think that David accuses God here.

As a second, and more preferable, reason, I think God's unjust demands did not surprise David. Rather, it appears as nothing unusual to David (and perhaps to the writer of the passage) that YHWH would tempt David to do something sinful and subsequently call that sinful act to account. David appears to *expect* that kind of behavior from YHWH. After all, as king, David certainly ruled in a similar fashion. No one could say that David's rule was consistent or evenhanded. But, in contrast to YHWH, even David probably had *cause* for his unpredictable, violent behavior. Often when David acts violently, we may ascribe his behavior to excessive ambition and uncontrolled appetites.[14] But the portrayal of God in this passage gives no motivations for divine behavior.

This is similar to, but to be distinguished from, the idea of YHWH encouraging sinful behavior in order to *test* the people and see if they will obey.[15] For instance, when God ordered Abraham to sacrifice his child, we are told that God was "testing" Abraham and had no intention of seeing the wicked deed carried out. This is similar to a test in Shakespeare's *Macbeth*, where Malcolm, the king apparent after the death of the ruling king, tests McDuff by appearing to be evil, to see if McDuff would follow an evil king. McDuff refuses and is deemed worthy. This census passage is not such a test. There is no sense that had David refused, he would have "passed" the test. In this instance, God makes a calculated effort to draw the people into wicked behavior.

If the people had not sinned by submitting to a census, then YHWH would have failed and would have been sorely disappointed. It was the will of YHWH that YHWH's people violate the will of YHWH! And then when they obeyed the will of YHWH by sinning, YHWH punished them for violating the divine will! In a test, if the subject refused to sin, that would constitute a successful resolution to the ordeal—one would therefore "pass" the test. But David cannot pass any test here. He will disobey God if he *refuses* to take the census. He will disobey God *by* taking the census.

But the "god problem" cannot be removed by a simple substitution as attempted by the Chronicler, to exonerate YHWH from complicity in the crime of the census. In Chronicles, the sinful enticement is meted out by one personage (Satan) already regarded as evil. YHWH is presumably righteous. But the punishment, by its scope, appears worse than the crime! The theological problems in this passage continue to accumulate.

David's Choice: Pestilence, Famine, or Military Defeat

YHWH gives David a choice of punishments, perhaps as a concession to divine complicity in the act. Such a choice appears as a boon to David, although as the options unfold, each one seems more horrible than the last.[16]

> When David rose in the morning, the word of the LORD came to the prophet Gad, David's seer, saying, "Go and say to David: Thus says the LORD: 'Three things I offer you; choose one of them, and I will do it to you.' " So Gad came to David and told him; he asked him, "Shall three years of famine come to you on your land? Or will you flee three months before your foes while they pursue you? Or

> shall there be three days' pestilence in your land? Now
> consider, and decide what answer I shall return to the one
> who sent me. (2 Sam. 24:11–13)

The three choices successively offer a decrease in duration as
they increase in destruction and death of the punishment. They
also increase in the level of YHWH's direct involvement. Sick-
ness implies the fullest level of divine activity. The random ter-
ror of disease, striking without warning and seemingly
without regard for the character of the person, has always been
a major cause of metaphysical shock and a dramatic sign of
divine displeasure. Disease was regarded as a direct act of
YHWH, because the stricken subject seemingly was attacked
by invisible forces, and randomly.

In the film *Hannah and Her Sisters,* Woody Allen plays a character who thinks he has a brain tumor. Despite all the answers
that science can provide, the character still plunges into a religious crisis as he tries to deal with his impending suffering and
death. It comes upon this modern everyperson in the same way
it came upon the ancient Israelite, suddenly and without warning, unmerciful and uncaring. In a world that contains such
horrors, what can one believe in?

David's choice is decidedly theological—he chooses that punishment which places him *most directly* in the hands of YHWH.
And this part of the passage lies in tension with the problems of
the opening line, which tells of the anger of God. After everything
that has taken place, YHWH's hands are the last place *I* would
want to go. Anything would be preferable to that! But David inexplicably chooses complete dependence upon the direct force of
YHWH's anger over any of the more mediated actions.

Two of the choices, three months of famine and three days
of plague, are both natural disasters, regarded as of divine orig-
ination. One can only speculate as to why David regarded the
famine as less directly associated with God than the plague.

Perhaps it has something to do with the attempt at distancing YHWH theologically from the weather deities (Ba'al being the Canaanite storm god), or perhaps disease just seemed more personal to the Israelites than weather. Famine might be caused by warfare, in which case its initial cause would be human efforts. Or, as it has been suggested, famine is more a result of God's neglect than God's anger.[17]

But the choice turned out to be more horrible than David had expected. Both YHWH and David ultimately marvel at the excessiveness of the punishment. Second Samuel offers two versions of how the plague ended. In the first version, when YHWH sees the destruction approach Jerusalem, he instructs the angel to cease killing the population:

> But when the angel stretched out his hand toward Jerusalem to destroy it, the LORD relented concerning the evil, and said to the angel who was bringing destruction among the people, "It is enough; now stay your hand." (2 Sam. 24:16)

In the second version, it is David who initiates the cessation:

> When David saw the angel who was destroying the people, he said to the LORD, "I alone have sinned, and I alone have done wickedly; but these sheep, what have they done? Let your hand, I pray, be against me and against my father's house. (2 Sam. 24:17)

These two alternate endings of the plague cannot be harmonized. However, they both express the horror when the key figures (YHWH, David) realize the magnitude of their responsibility for the carnage. When seventy thousand were struck down with plague and bodies piled up everywhere, David had to put his foot down and say "enough!" Previously, he had not been struck by the manifest unfairness of being punished for obeying an expressed desire of YHWH, but the rising death tolls spurred him to oppose the onrushing wrath of God. Why not earlier? What line had YHWH crossed that finally compelled David to stand up to divine action?

David objects when he begins to fear that YHWH's destruction will encompass the entirety of the people that his officials had counted! How ironic that the very count by which David intended to increase his power now becomes invalid because of the epic disaster that was eating away the numerical strength of Israel. David had to say stop before he became a king over nothing. Additionally, David becomes angry at the magnitude of the punishment and the innocence of its victims. What David could accept in abstract theological terms (YHWH sending a three-day plague) in reality was simply too horrible to continue without protest.

This massively upsetting and disorienting story then becomes linked in 1 Samuel to an altar erected by David on the threshing floor of Arauna, and for the Chronicler it is linked to the most sacred site in the royal traditions of Israel, the site of the Solomonic Temple. This site is also sacred to Christians because some major events in the life of Jesus and the apostles are said to have taken place there. For Muslims, the Dome of the Rock marks the last resting place of Mohammed's feet before he rose into heaven. The possession of that site is now shared by the Muslims (the Dome of the Rock) and the Jews (the Wailing Wall). But doesn't it appear counterproductive to use such a troubling, ambiguous passage to validate such an important site? I would have picked a less ambivalent and more God-worshiping passage, rather than a passage that brings to question the very integrity and morality of the divine being.

Obviously, this geographical linkage indicates how seriously the ancient Israelites took this passage. However, soon afterward the story was defanged by the Chronicler and ignored by virtually everybody else. It certainly finds small welcome in lectionaries. But at some point in their history, Israel regarded this story as intimately related to the cultic and liturgical life of Israel. The site of the centralized temple was sanctified by the culminating event of this story. This site was believed to be the actual place where the hand of YHWH's anger ceased to slaughter the Israelites.

Implied is that death moved upon the Israelites as an on-rushing cloud, as when the shadow of a cloud travels over the land at the wind's speed. How horrible that would be, to see death approach in such a fashion, first in the town down the road, and then in the houses of your neighbors, and finally in your house, engulfing you and then passing beyond you. No wonder they would regard the actual space where the death was halted with a kind of hushed reverence.

But what might they have thought of when they connected their temple with such a historical event? Did they think that *this* was the kind of God to which they were building their temple and that the cult of the Jerusalem Temple was primarily to slake the anger of such a God, which otherwise was liable to break out again against Israel at any moment? The Temple, then, would be understood as an attempt to install layers of ritual and cultic officials between this dangerous God and the people, *to protect the people from YHWH*. In such a case, it is obvious how this story became the *raison d'être* for the Temple.

Certainly, though, that strongly contrasts with the pro-nouncement of YHWH's faithfulness and consistency toward Israel, a text that is placed as part of Solomon's prayer of dedi-cation to the newly built Temple:

> O YHWH, God of Israel, there is no God like you in heaven above or on earth beneath, keeping covenant and steadfast love for your servants who walk before you with all their heart, the covenant that you kept for your servant my father David as you declared to him; you promised with your mouth and have this day fulfilled with your hand. (1 Kings 8:23–24)[18]

Have we uncovered an ancient controversy, an attempt on the part of some of the tradents to suppress the dangerous aspects of God in favor of a more domesticated version? Or do we find two different views of the Temple? And two views of what its purpose was in the hearts of the people—and ultimately how they were to regard their god?

DAVID'S GOD, ISRAEL'S GOD

Thus, in this passage, deity is portrayed negatively, and the story becomes linked to the most sacred site in Israel. Later tradents did not refer to this, so we might conclude that the story's theological function fell out of fashion very quickly. But we must ask, "Can we gain an understanding of what that function might have been?" And further, "May the story have any possible meaning for the contemporary reader beyond merely satisfying antiquarian curiosities?" Why would anyone want, or feel compelled, to regard the deity as unpredictable and morally questionable, as God is portrayed in this passage?

One possibility is that belief in a vindictive God supported the ruling structure. Perhaps those in power enjoined worship of a dangerous deity as a means of social control. The argument would go something like this: This God is dangerous. We must appease the anger of this God. We (the cultic leaders) are the exclusive interpreters of the will of this God. Therefore, do everything we tell you.

I don't, however, believe this was the case. Such negative portrayals of deity were threatening to the social order, not supportive of the status quo. Rather, since the leaders derived their authority from God, it was to their advantage that the people regard deity as perfect and not to be questioned.

The notion that whatever God does is by definition righteous is not a logical necessity, but rather a political one that provides support for those who hold the reins of power. The opposite position, which almost *requires* that God be questioned and judged, represents the voice of a de-centered Israel. Such a God, this story seems to say, must be questioned, must be challenged. And, further, there is really nothing that we could do to be certain that God will be pleased. Therefore, this passage leads us to question not only deity but the entire apparatus of a cult that is designed to appease God (which is ironic since the passage is so inextricably linked to the cult). This God might require the very things that YHWH hates and be the cause of further sin and punishment. Thinking along these lines creates skeptics and rebels.

People worshiped YHWH, so construed, because the activities of such a god *accorded with their experience*. The things ancient peoples suffered were frequently sudden, unexplained. This is a formulation of the old theodicy debate. Either God is not responsible, because of human free will or some contrary supernatural force (Satan, or some other deity), or, as in this narrative, God is responsible, and then either human pain *is* evil or else it only *seems* to be evil. If human pain is truly evil, then God is construed as being partly evil—sometimes God might be guilty of evil acts.

Is it more of a comfort to know that a god who cannot always be trusted causes the bad things that happen, or to worship a god of severely limited power? It is a tough choice. The Israelites were never able to agree. What comfort is there in knowing that the god you worship, however evil, is in fact the most powerful god, that everything that happens to you, for good and for ill, is the direct result of divine intervention? I think the belief that God was the most powerful of the deities was important but was not the primary payoff of this story. More importantly, when one construes God as having certain key features, there come certain inevitable (though often unforeseen) consequences. A powerful, proactive deity might be necessary for certain kinds of prayers and rituals, but with that deity comes the negative, that is, a deity that must be held responsible when not acting benevolently. To reject a god who causes diseases, might, by implication, mean a rejection of a god who is behind and somehow embodied by chaos, by randomness, by the dark inchoate forces of creativity. Julia Kristeva, European philosopher, called this chaos the *chora*, the cosmic, maternal womb that both gives us birth and consumes us. Hindu thought understands this too with the multi-armed Shiva who both creates and destroys, and is the source of all creativity. What I am suggesting is that when we eliminate the god who causes disease, or even worse, the god who causes disease *and* promotes sin (as most Western religious traditions have done), we might also lose the god who created Blake's burning Tyger:

> Tyger, Tyger burning bright
> in the forests of the night,
> What immortal arm or hand,
> shaped thy fearful symmetry?

Blake marvels at the terrible power and grace of the wild, jungle "tyger." He realized as well that to posit a divine being who could create such a frightening creature threatens his nice, orderly universe. Blake finally questions, "Did he who made the lamb make thee?"

Nadab and Abihu, Martyrs:
The *Dangerous* God
(Leviticus 10)

Shardik was a great bear, a god, in the novel by Richard Adams. For many years the god would not appear, and a community of priestesses guarded the memory of Shardik. As the story opens, a great bear has appeared in the woods. The question is raised, how can we know if this is truly Shardik, or just a bear? The priestesses, obedient to their calling, move into the woods to minister to their god. They locate the enormous bear and begin to feed and groom the wild beast. Sometimes the bear would submit to their ministrations, but other times, without warning, the bear would turn and tear the face off one of the women, crush another.[1]

The charm of Adams's book is his ability to make the theological concern of this savage community our own. They questioned whether this was "just" a savage bear whose fury could break out at any time, or a god, whose every move must be interpreted as the divine will. It has long been my conviction that in the Hebrew Bible we frequently encounter YHWH, the God of Israel, in the same way that those primitives encountered Shardik. And this observation raises the question, both in the novel and in the following Israelite narratives, What sort of god was this to believe in? We might further ask of these Israelite stories, How does such a belief or ideology reflect larger societal concerns, and how did belief in such a god shape the society?

Stated plainly, my thesis is that the Israelite writers frequently depicted YHWH as a dangerous, unpredictable force liable to break out in violence with no warning or provocation. And the story of Nadab and Abihu in Leviticus 10 speaks directly to this issue.

THE PROBLEM AND ITS CONTEXT

Briefly, Nadab and Abihu were priests, recently ordained, in the newly established sanctuary, the tent of meeting. They offered incense within the sanctuary, mixing it with "strange fire" (Lev. 10:1, KJV). The "strange fire" remains unspecified, but the narrator states that YHWH had not commanded this offering. A flash of fire explodes out of the altar[2] and incinerates the two young men. While their steaming bodies lie there, their elders, Aaron their father, and Moses their uncle, debate the meaning of the event and the proper disposition of the bodies.

Moses, leader of Israel, and his younger brother Aaron, the high priest, reacted differently to the violent deaths. Moses pronounces an enigmatic statement, with only a dubious connection to what had taken place. "It's just like the Lord said: 'I will be sanctified by those who draw near [that is, the priests], and all the people will glorify me' " (Lev. 10:3, author's translation). In its narrative context here, it suggests a *human* sacrifice, which accomplishes the sanctification of God. Aaron, for his part, remains silent.

Nadab and Abihu offered strange fire, and fire burst forth from the altar and consumed them. But doesn't that make YHWH's fire stranger than the fire of the young priests?—a fire that breaks some cultic infraction versus a fire that consumes human flesh? Edward Greenstein, a Jewish critic of scripture and midrash, claims that it is easily as difficult to understand YHWH's motivations as it is to understand whatever motivated Nadab and Abihu to present that incense offering.[3] Kirschner, a Rabbinics scholar, notes:

> the fire that consumed Nadab and Abihu [is] the same favorable fire which confirmed Noah's sacrifice, marked Solomon's consecration of the Temple, and consumed Elijah's sacrifice on Mt. Carmel; it is also the same fire which will descend again when the Temple is rebuilt in messianic times.[4]

The passage disturbs.[5] Greenstein has described it as "a punishment in search of a crime."[6] What did they do to deserve such a punishment? What was this strange fire? Are we supposed to be satisfied with the simple pronouncement that YHWH had not commanded such an offering? Are we compelled to say that because this was not part of YHWH's explicit instructions regarding proper worship of himself in the sanctuary, YHWH was justified in executing them through immolation?

These disturbing questions drive me in two directions seeking resolution. I search intertextually for a wider context by which we might understand the mysteries in Leviticus 10.[7] Then I examine carefully the text itself. Is it a warning to priests against liturgical innovation or perhaps a subtle protest against divine violence? Traces embedded in the text suggest how subsequent readers interpreted this narrative.

The Wider Context and Transition

The first nine chapters of Leviticus depict the ordination of Aaron's family, the sanctification of the tent of meeting, and miscellaneous instructions on sacrifices and offerings. That Aaron *and* his two sons were ordained to the priesthood there can be no question. Biblical critic N. H. Snaith and others have claimed that Nadab and Abihu were destroyed because only their father Aaron had been ordained priest and only Aaron could make the offerings on behalf of Israel.[8] But from the very first chapter Aaron's sons are included in every stage of the cult. "If Nadab and Abihu were indeed qualified to approach the altar as priests, it may be surmised that their offense turned on procedure."[9] For example, the first chapter of Leviticus (Lev. 1:7, 8) says, "The sons of the priest Aaron shall put fire on the altar and arrange wood on the fire. Aaron's sons the priests shall arrange the parts. . . . "[10] The actual ordination of the two sons is recorded in Leviticus 8.

The ordination ceremony took seven days to complete, and during that time YHWH specified many special sacrifices and rituals. Probably the high point occurred on the eighth day when Aaron and his sons, now fully qualified, presented on behalf of the people the threefold sacrifice—the sin offering, the burnt offering, and the offering of well-being (Lev. 9:22)—upon the altar.

> Then Moses brought Aaron and his sons forward, and washed them with water. . . . And Moses brought forward Aaron's sons, and clothed them with tunics, and fastened sashes around them, and tied headdresses on them. . . . He led forward the bull of sin offering; and Aaron and his sons laid their hands upon the head of the bull of sin offering. . . . Then he brought forward the second ram, the ram of ordination. Aaron and his sons laid their hands on the head of the ram. . . . (Lev. 8:6, 13, 14, 22)

YHWH ignited the fire upon the altar and revealed his glory. The people responded to the theophany by shouting and prostration. A priestly tradition that will be important for the subsequent narrative assumes that this fire, divinely enkindled, remained burning on the altar perpetually[11]—the "holy fire" that will be distinguished from the "strange fire" of Nadab and Abihu. The writer of Leviticus distinguishes the two fires, and in that difference rests the treatment of the two hapless priests.

Other Examples of Incense and Instructions to Priests

In an effort to solve the mystery of this "strange fire," some have looked to the incense as the source of the offense.[12] Certainly, in Exodus 30 Aaron is told: "You shall make an altar on which to offer incense. . . . You shall not offer unholy incense on it" (Ex. 30:1, 9, NRSV). The phrase "unholy incense" represents the Hebrew words *qetoret zarah;* "strange fire" is *'es zarah.* But should we identify the "unholy incense" (*zarah,* "strange") of Exodus 30 with the "strange fire"? And what is meant by "strange" in either case? Biblical critic Gnana Robinson states that "the context [Exodus 30] may show that these phrases 'strange fire' and 'strange incense' are synonymous, and that they both refer to the same thing, namely, the worship of 'strange gods.'"[13]

Heinisch, a biblical critic in the 1930s, observes that the offense cannot have been their failure to bring the fire from the altar, for this they had not been commanded to do; nor can their offense have been a failure to follow the prescriptions of Exodus 30:34–38 in the preparation of the incense. The prescription in Exodus must be a relatively late insertion, these ingredients being obviously unobtainable in the days of the wanderings in the wilderness. Nor can the offense have been that Nadab and Abihu took it upon themselves to enter the most holy place, for they did not do this. It is argued, therefore, that the offense lay in their thought to bring an offering of incense on their own initiative and without the authority of Moses or of Aaron.[14]

When the sons of Korah, Levites but not priests, struggled for authority against Moses and Aaron (Numbers 16), Moses commanded them to offer incense. When they brought the censors to the sanctuary, the earth opened and swallowed them up. Clearly the sons of Korah were punished for their rebellion against the authority of Moses and Aaron, for their demand to be priests. After they were destroyed, Moses told Aaron to kindle *his* censor with fire from the sacrificial altar (Num. 16:46), so perhaps the sons of Korah had been tricked into bringing "strange fire" into the sanctuary precincts, that is, fire not from the perpetually burning altar, presumably the source of "holy fire." We may contrast with this the order given by Moses to Aaron in Numbers 16:46: "Take your censer, put fire on it *from the altar*." Therefore we may conclude that licit fire is fire from the altar and that the incense is not bad. The source of fire is the question.[15]

The Old Testament includes other incidents regarding cultic infractions with incense. King Jeroboam offers incense at his newly reestablished shrine at Bethel. A man of God from Judah appears to condemn both the king and the altar of sacrifice he sought to consecrate. Jeroboam's offense appears to have little to do with the incense itself, suggesting little connection with the prohibition in Exodus 30.[16] Either the Deuteronomist identifies his wickedness with the establishment of sanctuaries that rival the Solomonic Temple in Jerusalem, or else as king he was usurping priestly prerogatives, as did King Saul. In either case, after the king offers incense, the focus shifts to the sacrificial altar, and incense is not mentioned again.

King Uzziah grew proud and offered incense in the Temple.[17] The priests rebuked him, saying, "It is not for you, Uzziah, to make offering to the LORD, but for the priests the descendants of Aaron, who are consecrated to make offering" (2 Chron. 26:18). YHWH struck King Uzziah with leprosy for his transgression of the priestly prerogative. Note Saul's decline when he tries to act like a priest (1 Samuel 13) in the battle of Michmash, although David seems to be able to offer sacrifices with impunity (e.g., 2 Samuel 6—directly after the incident with Uzzah). Whether a king was permitted to act like a priest seems directly related to the king's authority over the priestly class, and the trouble a king had with such activities was a direct result of the power possessed by the priestly faction in the royal court.[18]

Other Incidents of Ritual Misfire

In another example of "ritual misfire,"[19] when both Cain and Abel offered sacrifice, there was something wrong with Cain's offering and YHWH did not accept it. Cain did not suffer immolation, but there were consequences just the same.[20] That Cain protested the unfairness of the punishment, and by implication also protested the rejection of his sacrifice, suggests that a similar response to the punishment of Nadab and Abihu might also be possible.

Not surprisingly, in the liturgical calendar of Judaism, the Haftorah for the Nadab and Abihu passage is the shocking death of Uzzah (2 Samuel 6). When he tried to steady the cart that carried the ark of the covenant, "God struck him there . . . and he died there beside the ark of God."[21] The story closes with David's horrified reaction. He expressed both anger and fear, naming the place Perez-Uzzah, which may be translated as "Uzzah's attacker." In David's conception, YHWH lurks as an aggressive, demonlike figure, ready to strike out against anyone. In both of these passages, God strikes out against seemingly innocent people who appeared to mean well.

TRACES OF PROTEST WITHIN LEVITICUS 10

The Strange Fire of Nadab and Abihu

If we are to understand the story, we must develop some theories as to the motivation of the two young men and some idea of what is the nature of the strange fire.[22]

The theories regarding motivation fall into three categories. (1) They offered profane fire, that is, kitchen or oven fire. They are therefore guilty of laziness (not wanting to start a new fire), or carelessness (they didn't know it mattered). (2) They deliberately offended God, committing the crime of sacrilege, an attempt to in some way undermine YHWH's authority, perhaps offering fire from the altar of another god. Biblical critic John Hartley asserts: "At the minimum they were trying to incorporate some pagan ritual dear to them into the cult of YHWH."[23] In this second possibility, the offense involved is not profane fire (secular fire) but holy fire from a rival altar. In the first theory, the brothers are inconsequential dolts who inadvertently cross in front of an angry bear, who then tears their bodies to pieces; in this second theory, they are Promethean rebels against divine authority. (3) Some describe Nadab and Abihu as mad mystics, deliberately immolating themselves in the divine glory, intoxicated with the promise of the *kavod*, and thus sanctifying the sanctuary by their devotion.[24] Greenstein summarizes Philo's interpretation: "The young priests in a fit of ecstasy purposely transgressed the danger limit of the divine presence so that they would be immolated and translated into immortality, like Enoch and Elijah."[25]

Texts are polysemous, and a narrative such as this one raises far more questions than it resolves. However, in spite of the many voices raised to explain the source of motivation for the two priests, to me one reconstruction appears stronger than the others and, to be honest, suits my purpose better. Were Nadab and Abihu venal or just careless? Was the strange fire simply badly mixed or incorrect incense inappropriate for this particular ritual? Or was it a deliberate offering to a non-Israelite god?[26] I suggest the following reconstruction:

> Nadab and Abihu were young, excited at the prospects of cultic service in the new sanctuary. There were many things to learn and little time to learn it. Their father Aaron, burdened with the responsibility of the consecration ceremony, had little time to supervise the boys, but the eight-day ceremony was almost at a close.
>
> How exciting to be a priest, to earn the admiration and respect of the people![27] They were eager to serve YHWH, perhaps too eager.[28] In their enthusiasm, they offered incense in an unspecified way, drawing fire not from the altar but from a "secular" fire, a cooking fire perhaps. This was the transgression that resulted in otherwise qualified priests running afoul of the divine presence. Their cultic initiative was uncalled for, and their carelessness about mixing sacred and profane fires inexcusable.[29]

Certain aspects of the story, however, shatter the seeming clarity of this interpretation. First of all, as Greenstein points out, the word "fire" is mentioned twice: "[they] each took his censer, put fire [*'es*] in it, and laid incense on it; and they offered unholy fire [*'es zarah*] before the LORD." Many translate the first mention of fire as "coals," which doesn't address the problem at all. Greenstein notices here a crack in the text out from which meaning confronts the reader:

> The presupposition that there is a reason not only motivates the search (the reader already "knows" that some explanation lurks within the text); it necessarily posits or superimposes the structure of sin and punishment on the story. . . . The narrative of Nadav and Avihu meant to challenge or subvert the absolute rationality of the Torah, the scrutability of divine retribution.[30]

The explanation of the strange fire is not available in the text, although it would have been relatively simple for the narrator to provide an explanation. The phrase "strange fire" is *deliberately obscure!* So a solution that does not take into account this purposeful obfuscation is not a complete solution. The fact that so many different kinds of explanations are offered presents sufficient evidence for one to doubt a facile, all-embracing solution.

Moses' Pronouncement and Aaron's silence

Interpretive cues within the passage itself, reactions of the observers or participants, often provide important clues to inform a reading. As stated above, Moses the uncle and Aaron the father are given lines that comment on the events that have taken place. Moses says:

> This is what YHWH meant when he said,
>
>> "Through those who are near me
>>> I will show myself holy,
>> and before all the people
>>> I will be glorified. (Lev. 10:3)

Ambiguities abound in this pronouncement! First, the reader wonders, When exactly did YHWH make this statement to which Moses refers? Some suggest that what we have here is an obscure proverb that Moses connects with this incident.[31] Others see Moses functioning prophetically: YHWH makes the pronouncement at the moment when Moses says it. Additionally, Greenstein speculates that YHWH's actions in killing Nadab and Abihu are YHWH's speech—YHWH spoke by sending forth that fire.[32]

But what does the statement mean? It can have a positive or a negative sense. Those who draw near are clearly the priests, those who have the privilege of drawing near the sanctuary. But how exactly is YHWH shown holy by those who draw near, that is, the priests? First, in an absolute sense, the ministry of the priests intends the "sanctification" of YHWH, that is, the behavioral demonstration of his holiness. This pronouncement appears to be the culmination of the story in the same way that a "pronouncement" is the point of Jesus' "pronouncement stories." When the pronouncement is placed in its narrative context, the words translated "made holy" take on a more ominous ring. Peretz Segal suggests that the verbs *kabod* (to glorify) and *qadesh* (to make holy) "are used as synonyms for divine retribution. It is the priests' job to render the holiness of God, but those priests who offend YHWH will be subject to divine retribution, which also demonstrates God's holiness."[33]

Moses thus approves of the divine judgment upon his nephews. "It serves them right!" we might imagine Moses saying. "YHWH is perfectly justified in what he has done!" To say such a thing to a parent whose children have just been destroyed before his eyes is insensitive to the extreme.

Aaron's reaction is at the same time much more profound and more enigmatic. He remains silent. Between Moses' verbosity and insensitivity and Aaron's silence is a gaping chasm. As this resonant silence echoes through many different reading communities, diverse explanations have been suggested. Some have seen in Aaron's silence a hearty approval of YHWH's righteous action in slaughtering his two sons. Baruch Levine notes that Aaron "accepted God's harsh judgement and did not cry out or complain at his painful loss.[34] Bernard Bamberger observes, "in the rabbinic phrase, he 'acknowledged the justice of the decree.' "[35] Others have seen an Aaron in bitter resignation or else active rebellion.[36]

There is a later exchange between Moses and Aaron in the same chapter of Leviticus. Moses reprimands Aaron for the improper handling of a particular sacrifice. They were supposed to eat it in the sacred tent, but instead they had burned the entire animal outside the tent. Moses says this to a man who, along with his remaining two sons, is trying to rebuild the shambles of his life and his priestly vocation. Aaron snaps back at Moses, sharp in his bitter anger, "Are you crazy? YHWH has just killed my two sons, and now I'm going to eat his sacrifice? And that way he would kill my whole family. Is that what you want?"[37] And this time Moses said nothing, realizing finally how inappropriate he had been.[38]

The reversal in the talkativeness in the two brothers suggests that the narrator does not give unreserved approval to the original statement of Moses. Aaron's silence becomes Moses' silence. Aaron usurps Moses' role as final arbiter of cultic behavior. Moses works from the perspective of the stringent rules of the cult. Aaron works from the perspective of family relationship. For Moses, all that YHWH does is good. For Aaron, YHWH is dangerous, and the rules must be bent a bit to avoid further dangerous contact with YHWH.

CONCLUSION

Imagine Moses and Aaron discussing theology over the steaming bodies of Nadab and Abihu—Moses' self-righteous pontification and Aaron's stony, enigmatic silence. In a sense, these two literary figures, Moses and Aaron, represent the two distinct Israelite responses to the theological challenge of human pain and suffering. One group saw suffering as chiefly deserved pain, whether deserved because of membership in a certain non-Israelite group, or, if within the camp of Israel, because of personal or corporate transgressions. This point of view was overwhelmingly dominant in ancient Israel.

The other response, linked to Aaron's silence, contains two affirmations: (1) that the Israelite God is responsible for all things, whatever happens; and (2) that everything that takes place (caused by God) is not good. Some acts of God must be refused. Failing that, they must be met with protest or open rebellion. Some see a temporal progression, one from the other—that in early Israel, the people believed in a violent unpredictable God, liable to break out against them without warning. The later Israelites, more sophisticated no doubt, believed in a god both benevolent and consistent. There is not sufficient evidence, however, to sustain the claim that these two theological attitudes could not have coexisted within the same society.[39]

It must have been difficult to sustain, on the one hand, the belief that God was most powerful, as well as believing that God was good. The belief in a dangerous god was one of the ways ancient Israelites solved that problem—God portrayed as a killer of innocents; a blind, idiot God; a force or power; energy like electricity (Nadab and Abihu were killed because they ignorantly touched a live wire without insulated gloves). Such passages portray the holiness of God as the blind irrationality of God's justice—you get in his way, even accidentally, and you get whacked.

In the book *Shardik* there is a recurring question whether the great bear was in fact a dumb animal or the great Bear god. That blind forces exist which can better us and terrify us there is no doubt. We may give this force a face and call it God (and thus God will terrify us).[40] The universe is presented to us with its random acts of violence, suffering, and death, and we must choose.

Either God commits these random acts of violence and cannot be trusted—this is what we find in the Nadab and Abihu stories—or else there are forces beyond even God's control. In Leviticus 10 we encounter a willingness to credit YHWH with causing some of the most painful things humans have ever experienced. Thus we encounter a despicable God. The narrator saw a greater risk in God being compromised than in his being despised.

The Bloody Bridegroom:
The *Malevolent* God
(Exodus 4:24–26)

On the way, at a place where they spent the night, YHWH met him and tried to kill him. But Zipporah took a flint and cut off her son's foreskin, and touched his genitals [lit., feet] with it, and said, 'Truly you are a bridegroom of blood to me!" So he let him alone. It was then she said, "a bridegroom of blood" with reference to circumcision.

Exodus 4:24–26, NRSV with modifications

Biblical scholars love this passage *because* it is totally incomprehensible. The pronouns have no antecedents. Whom did YHWH attack, Moses or his son? Upon whose "feet" (or "genitals")[1] did Zipporah cast her son's foreskin—those of Moses, the son, or YHWH? Further, interpreters have no idea of the meaning of the term "bloody bridegroom" (*ḥatan-damim*).[2] I assume that the blood referred to in the phrase would be the same blood placed on one of the characters' "feet," the blood shed in the circumcision. But no clear candidate emerges to identify as the bridegroom. Neither Moses, his son, nor YHWH fits very well the range of meanings for the Hebrew word *ḥatan*, translated here as "bridegroom."[3] And, since verse 26b ("It was then she said, 'a bridegroom of blood' in reference[4] to circumcision") claims to be an interpretation of the entire passage, understanding this phrase is indispensable.

There are other imponderables in the passage, some of

which I will discuss later, but all of which combine to make for an incomprehensible text, one in which key bits of information appear to be lacking, lost either accidentally in its transmissional history[5] or by design. Each interpreter who has taken up the challenge seeks a key to unlock the mysteries, whether from (most recently) the field of linguistics, comparative anthropology, or some more refined method of literary criticism.[6]

But sometimes a quest for clarity runs counter to a full appreciation of a biblical passage. The scientific model, where theories are proposed and then tested, and proven either valid or invalid on the basis of evidence, might not operate well on such literature. Jewish Midrash may well offer a more appropriate model for understanding this text. In the early centuries of the common era, the rabbis opened up and expanded the meaning of biblical texts by rewriting them, filling in the gaps with their imagination and erudition. Further, they brought two or more disparate texts together and allowed their juxtaposition to create new categories of meaning. Some of these texts might have *deliberately* alluded to another, but that didn't matter. Rather, the readers of Midrash demanded creativity and relevance from their commentaries.

And so we can see a multitude of Midrash-type commentaries and interpretations on this passage, emerging as different readers encounter this text. In the following general survey of reading strategies and results, I will not so much be examining which ones are correct, but rather exploring the different directions readings of this text have taken.

COMMENTARIES ON THE PASSAGE

Verse 26b—the Earliest Commentary

Verse 26b is the earliest written interpretation of this text. The first clue that this was not part of the original story is its repetition of the earlier phrase.[7] In verse 25 Zipporah says, "You are a bridegroom of blood to me." Verse 26 adds "A bridegroom of blood with reference to circumcision." The second is an explanatory gesture, an effort to shed light on a phrase that was already obscure at the time when verse 26b was added.[8] So the editor likely added 26b so that circumcision would become the focus.[9] The original story without 26b had circumcision as an element but did not make it the central concern of the text.[10] Previous to 26b, the story appears to recount how Zipporah wards off an attack by YHWH through three actions: (1) circumcision, (2) a painting of blood on the "feet" (genitals) of either Moses, their son, or YHWH, and (3) an obscure pronouncement ("bridegroom of blood"). The addition of this explanatory note in 26b suggests to subsequent readers (going through the three actions of Zipporah in order) that the *reason* for YHWH's attack was Moses' failure to circumcise. The blood painting/genital touching was a *sign* that circumcision had taken place, and that Zipporah's pronouncement addressed the issue of circumcision. None of these connections with circumcision was explicit within verses 24 or 25.[11] It might well have been that the three acts were connected efforts of Zipporah to ward off the god's anger, without reference to any *reason* that the god might be hostile.[12] One might then read this story either as a story of YHWH's anger turned aside by three ritual activities, without indicating *why* YHWH was angry, or as (along with 26b) a story of YHWH's vengeance against his chosen leader for violating the circumcision taboos.

As a result of this editorial activity by the writer of verse 26b, the earliest translations and paraphrases make explicit the connections between YHWH's anger and Moses' failure to circumcise.[13] The Septuagint (Greek) and Targums (Aramaic)[14] state clearly that Moses was the one attacked, that the reason for that attack was uncircumcision, either his own or his son's,[15] and that circumcision was the reason YHWH turned aside his attack when Zipporah performed the needed surgery.[16] There is great effort on the part of these early interpreters to deflect the horror of the story from God to some subsidiary angel or even demonic figure.[17]

Modern Interpretation

Until the nineteenth century, Jewish and Christian inter- preters continued the tradition of reading this as a circumci- sion story, although there was disagreement regarding who was attacked and who was circumcised. Then the whole sense of interpretation changed.[18] Modern scholars are willing to see this passage cut loose from its context in the book of Exo- dus, as well as its place in the Torah as a whole.[19] Genesis 17 gives an account of Abraham instituting the rite of circumci- sion to his extended family, circumcising himself, his son Ish- mael, and all the males in his household. The traditional way of reading Exodus 4:24–26 holds Moses responsible for know- ing this story. Therefore, in obedience to the covenant he should have circumcised himself and his son. By taking Exo- dus 4 out of this context, Genesis 17 (the story of Abraham) and Exodus 4 (the story of Moses) emerge as two rival ac- counts of the institution of the rite of circumcision.[20] This will- ingness to decontextualize Exodus 4:24–26, and even emend it to make more sense, results in four major theories, dis- cussed below.

1. The first theory focuses on the bridegroom story. The anomaly of referring to Moses (or some other figure) as a "bride- groom" has produced many explanations. Some suggest that the bridegroom designation makes sense if we emend the text, cutting out the character of the son.[21] The story might have orig- inally been a wedding night legend, explaining why bride- grooms had to be circumcised shortly before the wedding night.[22] Those who read the story in this way claim that the character of the son was a later interpolation by an anonymous editor who wrote at a time when circumcision was more cus-

tomarily performed in infancy. This story in its original context, it is claimed, was an explanation of the custom of circumcising young men shortly before their wedding.[23] Such a rite of cultic mutilation warded off, it was said, a "wedding demon" who would take the life of any bridegroom who was unprotected by the shedding of his genital blood.[24] When later Israelites instituted infant circumcision, the son was added and placed in its present context (at a point in the narrative long after Zipporah and Moses were married). In its original context, however, it was an etiology (origin story) explaining why bridegrooms had to be circumcised.[25]

Another wedding-night legend focuses on the supernatural threat to a couple on their wedding night. Biblical critic William Propp, in his survey of approaches to this text, notes the possibility that YHWH demanded to take sexually every virgin on or before her wedding night.[26] This story originally functioned as an account of some deity claiming its right to enjoy the first sexual favors of this budding Israelite bride.[27] In order to turn aside this supernatural ardor, the woman plays a trick, circumcising her husband and touching the god, convincing him that her hymen had been broken. The story would thus explain the tradition of circumcising bridegrooms on their wedding night.[28] Although an attractive theory, it remains implausibly motivated and ultimately not convincing.

2. Another theory holds that this story explained the etiology of infant circumcision and justified the shift in custom from circumcision as a puberty rite to one where it was performed upon infants.[29] When Zipporah circumcised her son and touched her husband's genitals with the bloody foreskin (as in one common reconstruction of the story), the ritual transference of the practice from adult to child was complete.[30] Henceforth, the society would not mandate bridegroom circumcision, but now infant circumcision would be required.[31]

3. To complicate things, many have noted that the Hebrew

word for bridegroom, *hatan,* is closely akin to an Arabic word translated "circumcision."[32] This has led to numerous explorations as to why the word or similar words might mean both circumcision and (in its various forms) different clan relations: bridegroom, son-in-law, brother-in-law, father-in-law. Study of this passage thus requires an analysis of the relationship of clan connections and circumcision. Julian Morgenstern suggests that at this particular point in the social development of Israel and pre-Israel, the people related through the mother and not the father's line. The brother-in-law, then, circumcised the new male into the clan.[33] So when Zipporah identifies someone in the narrative as a (*hatan-damim*), here translated "brother-in-law of blood," she is fulfilling some clan responsibility in the absence of her brother, bringing the new one under the matrilineal clan's protection and care.[34] Morgenstern therefore states, "hence the words spoken by Zipporah . . . mean no more than 'Verily one related by blood, i.e., the blood of the circumcision, art thou to me'; in other words, 'Verily thou art now a full member of my clan.' "[35] It should be noted that this perspective elides Moses from the story. The name Moses does not in fact occur anywhere in the three verses and must be inferred by the surrounding portions of Exodus.[36]

4. One of the most intriguing of the recent readings comes from Propp, who suggests that Moses was a bridegroom of blood because he had killed an Egyptian as a young man in Egypt. When he fled to Midian he carried bloodguilt with him (Ex. 2:11, 12). He marries Zipporah under false pretenses, and when they leave the asylum of Midian, moving back into the territory of the offended god, some punishing, supernatural agent who enforces the payment for bloodguilt attacks their family. Propp says it is

> Moses' attempt to return home with unexpiated blood-guilt upon him that elicits YHWH's attack . . . the pretext is the same: Moses had murdered an Egyptian. . . . Had

she known, she might have hesitated to marry a "bride-groom of blood-guilt" with both a price and a curse on his head. . . . Thus in ch. iv the surprise lies not in the Deity's attack in verse 25, but rather in his reassurances in verse 19: "Go return to Egypt, for all the men who seek your life have died."[37]

If it is the son who is struck, the story becomes remarkably similar to Bathsheba's loss of her first son with David, an infant attacked because of the bloodguilt of the father. Although Bathsheba's child does not survive the ordeal, Zipporah is able to save her child. So Zipporah does what she can to turn away divine anger, while at the same time she lashes out in anger against Moses, whose dishonesty set up this whole situation. "You bloody bridegroom!" she said. "You cursed man!" she spat out in derision. According to Propp,

> although YHWH commands Moses to return to Egypt [Ex. 4:19], he still holds him accountable for the death of the slain Egyptian. Zipporah sheds the blood of their son and dabs Moses' penis with it, thereby expiating her husband's sin. This ancient deed is supposedly why a circumcised child is called "bridegroom of bloodiness." Contrary to the view of almost all exegetes, [the Ex. 4:24–26 passage] is well integrated within the J narrative.[38]

YHWH, a character in this brief narrative, behaves strangely. Virtually every interpreter must in some way account for this anomaly. When one examines the story cut loose from its context in Exodus and the Torah, one finds that the character of YHWH in the narrative appears limited, unreliable, and even hostile.[39] This is not the God of Genesis 1, for instance—a God limitless in power and authority, an absolute monarch. Here God is more akin to the troll waiting under the bridge, or like Golum in J. R. R. Tolkien's *Lord of the Rings,* waiting in the shadows to attack nobility and steal what is good.

When taken in its context in Exodus, the behavior in this

passage is inconsistent with YHWH having just sent Moses on a mission. One marvels at how the same God would here attack that same man and his family, trying to kill him. Either one must ignore the context, or insist that something Moses did warranted such an extreme reaction.[40] Failing that, one must acknowledge a high degree of instability in the divine figure. Why would he now want to kill Moses? Explanations take the following general shapes. Some would ascribe such literature to a more primitive period in the history of Israel or of even pre-Israelite peoples, much more characteristic of a pagan world-view. Subsequent, more sophisticated writers in Israel, it is claimed, outgrew such ideas of deity. Others (and this represents the more traditional position) would justify YHWH's action by underscoring the heinousness of Moses' "crime" and the overwhelming importance of circumcision, thus claiming that YHWH's actions were justified.

This is always a troubling feature of the story, and one that will not go away unless we impose a more theologically correct picture of God upon our reading. The god of this story has often been described as "demonic" because he bursts upon them, attacking at night. Resemblance to other "night visitors" has often been noted, as for instance when Jacob wrestles with a man/angel.[41] In both cases, Exodus 4 and Genesis 32 (the Jacob story), the protagonist is attacked at night by a divine adversary.[42] The attack is turned aside, although not without injury, and the protagonist then goes on to a new stage of life.[43]

What many have characterized as a "primitive conception of the divine" is certainly localized, unstable, and downright hostile. I find it greatly doubtful that we can identify it as necessarily from an earlier era. I argue that such notions of God existed in all historical periods within ancient Israel (1100–100 B.C.E.) and reflected a significant minority perspective on the Israelite deity.

IMPONDERABLE ACTIONS,
IRREDUCIBLE CONFUSIONS

Failure of consensus on a given issue does not render the question moot or insoluble. However, in the case of this passage, the failure of consensus *is* significant: the key phrase in the story, *ḥatan-damim*, remains a cipher. It is not that it can mean *no*-thing. It can in fact mean many things; one might say *too* many things. Although insights from the Arabic *ḥtn* and from clan studies on Bedouin cultures and other similar tribal societies have enriched the understanding of the text, they have also multiplied its ambiguities. No one theory has proven strong enough to push the others out of consideration. There is no scholarly consensus on any of the key points. There remains, after more than a century of scholarly reflection, not to mention almost twenty-five hundred years of interpretive activity, no dominant or obvious way to understand this story.

Both Brevard Childs and Terence Fretheim—authors of commentaries on Exodus—bring us toward an understanding of the fundamental insolubility of this passage. Childs, in his discussion of *ḥatan-damim* ("bloody bridegroom") claims that the editor who inserted this story into its present context (the Yahwist?) had no idea what the phrase meant, and did not even attempt to define it, but instead associated it with the editor's own chief concern, circumcision. I quote from Childs:

> It seems evident that even when the story was being edited, the phrase 'blood-bridegroom' already presented problems. The comment . . . serves only to relate the enigmatic expression to the rite of circumcision. It is not at all clear that the redactor understood any longer what the phrase meant. His comment simply set it in relationship to the institution of circumcision. Whatever it meant, it belonged to the rite.[44]

Perhaps, Childs suggests, the reason the editor retained this story, while so many other characteristically pagan tales were probably destroyed by later monotheistic editors, was because of its concern for circumcision.[45]

From Fretheim we get the clearest statement yet as to how a conflicted text might produce meaning. He notes the ambiguity between two interpretive conclusions, circumcision of the husband or of the son. Fretheim suggests that both might be true in a blending of their identities in the story. He observes:

> in the absence of any unequivocal indication as to who it is that God tries to kill, interpretation should leave the matter open, moving with both possibilities, Moses and his (presumably firstborn) son. While most scholars think the object of God's action is Moses, his uncircumcised son would also be endangered in view of Gen. 17:14. If it is also the case that Moses had not been circumcised, and that the blood transferred the circumcision of his son to him, there is a fluidity of reference between Moses and his son that is difficult to sort out.[46]

I thereby offer the following observations: (1) There is no emerging consensus among the community of scholars regarding this passage. (2) There exists a traditional reading, held in common within the Jewish and Christian communities and held by many academics as well, that YHWH's attack was justified because of the serious nature of Moses' crime. And his crime was failure to circumcise either himself or his son, or both. (3) Most new scholars who approach the passage expect a new consensus to aggregate around their own thesis, with which they hope to provide the key that will make sense of the whole.

It is not just an accident or coincidence that no consensus has emerged regarding this passage.[47] Rather, it is because this passage is characteristically incomprehensible and, as such (given the human desire for wholeness, orderliness, and closure), it produces diverse meanings when interpreted by different readers in different reading communities. So, therefore, the way to "understand" this passage is to first accept its incomprehensibility. One can never really know who was attacked, who was circumcised, or what "bloody bridegroom" means. This is significant. I would venture that these imponderables and the fact of their incomprehensibility are the most important characteristics of this text. They compel us to experience the text in its mystery. What then happens to our understanding of God when we examine the imponderables *as* imponderables, and not puzzles to be solved and unlocked? Perhaps we must see such texts not as narratives but as a place where narratives are born, as stellar clouds, nebulas, where stars are born. A reader reads the text and produces a narrative that makes sense of the text for her.

In conclusion therefore, I offer two interpretations, twin stories. In one, warding off the wrath of a hostile deity provides the focus; in the other, circumcision is the key feature.

THE FIRST STORY

The deity waited on the way he knew Moses would come. He planned to spring out and surprise Moses, overpower him. YHWH focused his anger in the direction of his adversary and in no way intended to let him pass. Moses would not continue on his way to Egypt.

Moses came with his family, his wife and infant son. It didn't matter. It was Moses that the deity wanted. YHWH sprang out into the middle of the road from behind a tree, and struck Moses, who fell, coughing blood, in pain.

But Zipporah knew magic that could drive away a god. She put her son down on the ground, unwrapped him, and with a stone knife[48] cut off the baby's foreskin. While he screamed in shock and pain, she left the child, pulled up her husband's clothing and touched her husband's penis with the bloody piece of skin. She pronounced an incantation.

In shock and outrage, the god withdrew before he could kill Moses. He could not overcome the woman's powerful spell. It took Moses three days to be well enough to travel. They were not disturbed again.

THE SECOND STORY

Her father was a priest, for God's sake. Of course she knew about circumcision.[49] Moses insisted they delay the holy operation until they had reached their destination.[50] Making a deity wait for what belonged to it—never a good idea.

At roughly the midpoint in their journey, Moses fell terribly ill. She knew it; she knew some evil thing would happen to them because they had not placated YHWH, who was Moses' god and her father's god as well. She hoped it wasn't too late. She quickly and efficiently circumcised her son, and touched Moses' penis, in an effort to protect the two of them from an enraged deity. The sacrifice worked, for Moses recovered, and they were soon on their way.

In both stories God is other than what is found in the traditional formulations. The first is certainly a warding-off tale. In that story, God is localized, unstable, and hostile. We have here a picture of deity quite different from the one in traditional Jewish and Christian formulations. The God of this story is more characteristic of an older, tribal, pagan context, in which there are many gods of various dispositions, each ruling a particular region.

In the second story, Zipporah still faces an enraged deity who still needs to be placated with an act of ritual mutilation. The difference is that now the narrative justifies the actions of deity by giving them an explanation (Moses' failure to circumcise). Still, however, the god portrayed remains localized, unstable, and hostile.[51] In both cases God is malevolent. Did the Israelites *believe* in such a God, or did they use these narratives for some other purpose? Such narratives seem to provide a theological alternative to the prevailing notions of deity. Perhaps the Israelites frequently experienced God as malevolent. In the twentieth century, the genocidal century, this might not any longer seem unusual.

›6‹

The Mad Prophet and
the *Abusive* God
(2 Kings 2: 23–25)

Whenever a stranger enters our town, we tell the story of the Mad Prophet, who passed through our territory a long time ago. He had God with him. But he was a miserable, vain, nasty little man who destroyed our entire population of young boys, our whole next generation. Many, many women would have no husbands for at least a decade. All the people were terrified of him—tried to keep on his good side. You see, when those boys saw him coming, they knew who he was, but there was boldness in numbers and they began to tease him. He pronounced a solemn curse against them—he danced around and sung a strange and unpleasant song and sprinkled certain powders from a bag at his waist. The boys left the old man, still laughing at him. Maybe if they had just not mentioned his bald head, it would not have happened. It was bright red, burned in the sun.

Two bears came out, female I think, angry as hell. There was no reason for those bears to be so angry. They hadn't any cubs. We figure the prophet did it: he called down those bears, killed all our little boys. Those boys didn't mean anything by it. They were just being kids. Why did he have to call down those bears? Why did he have to make them so angry?

Why would God give that kind of power to that man?

Why would God do that, unless God was that way too, mean-spirited and vengeful, vain as any wealthy prince?

The preceding echoes 2 Kings 2:23–25. The full text is:

> He went up from there to Bethel; and while he was going up on the way, some small boys came out of the city and jeered at him, saying, "Go away, baldhead! Go away, baldhead!" When he turned around and saw them, he cursed them in the name of the LORD. Then two she-bears came out of the woods and mauled forty-two of the boys. From there he went on to Mount Carmel, and then returned to Samaria.

There are, of course, many other ways to read (and misread) this passage. When one examines the history of interpretation regarding this "puerile"[1] story, one finds that it has often been a place for strong arguments over interpretation, and it becomes apparent that much is at stake here. Frequently interpreters have ignored this admittedly brief passage or they have imposed outlandish interpretations to protect the reputation of YHWH. And that is my first point—that most interpretations of this passage are primarily "spin control."

If one emphasizes the heinousness of the children's crime, and frames the story in such a way that they *deserved* to be ripped apart by bears, then YHWH is exculpated. Ziolkowski observes that the passage

> reveal[s] a Western literary motif about male children that, stemming from a terse pericope in the Hebrew Bible, presents them as a sacrilegious type—ancient precursors to the "punks," "skinheads," and "wilding" youths who stalk the streets of modern metropolises . . . [and] always implies a kinship between boys, irreligiousness, and "evil," thereby subverting the virtual beatification of children traditionally embraced by Christianity.[2]

Some early Jewish interpretations suggested that the small boys were really young adults, deliberately attacking YHWH's authority by insulting the prophet because they loved idols.

> All that is necessary is to admit that the worthless spirit which prevailed in Bethel was openly manifested in the ridicule of the children, and that these boys knew Elisha, and in his person insulted the prophet of the Lord. If this was the case, then Elisha cursed the boys for the purpose of avenging the honour of the Lord, which had been injured in his person: and the Lord caused this curse to be fulfilled, to punish in the children the sins of the parents, and to inspire the whole city with a salutary dread of His holy majesty.[3]

Or perhaps it was not the children's fault, but rather the evil parents of Bethel who sent their children out deliberately to disparage the prophet because they did not want to worship YHWH; they wanted to sacrifice to idols. But why would they send their children out? As a sacrifice? Because they thought the children were immune to the prophet's curse? Didn't they believe the prophet was dangerous? Or were they deliberately trying to get him angry? I am not convinced that there was any such religious conspiracy or plot against Yahwism in the boys' mockery, or that they were *sent* to do evil work. Rather, they were mischievous, taunting a non-local grownup, just for the fun of it, and because they thought they wouldn't get caught.

Another effort to release us from the heavy oppression of this passage comes from historical criticism. This passage, it is claimed, derives from an early, tribal period in Israel's history. When interpreters use the word "tribal" they envision a more innocent time, more childlike, less sophisticated than our own.[4] Some see a tribal state as desirable and romantic; others see it as barbaric and uncivilized. But both views condescend toward any group so designated. Most important for our purposes, a position labeled "tribal" will usually mean a position our culture has transcended, like cannibalism, or blood sacrifice, or nudity. In this case, tribal means, "We can excuse these people for their primitive depictions of the prophets, and their hyper-literal view of the power of a curse, because we have outgrown such simplistic notions of deity. Our god is moral and would never do anything like this."

Another implication of the historical-critical approach to this passage is that it ignores the above-mentioned moral/theological questions entirely, and only asks what purpose this story served for a particular group that existed in the distant past? Most commonly, the commentaries suggest that the Elisha miracle stories, which have their own unique character within the larger literary units, come from oral tales first told in small regional, tribal groups.[5] They either promote the life and reputation of the prophet[6] or promote the region associated with that prophet.[7] Gray observes, "Those at various shrines associated with Elisha possibly compete with one another in the local miracles which they related of the prophet, until eventually the various local traditions were collected, combined and recorded in the Elisha-saga as we now have it."[8] Or the miracle stories are about the good old days when men were men and prophets were prophets. Such nostalgic storytelling serves to criticize the present days, when things are not so good.[9]

In these "primitive" readings, no one suggests that a rural, patriarchal culture would approve of YHWH's punishment of children. Patriarchal culture places its hope for the future upon the male children. And if that is so, then many interpretations (which assume that the putative original authors believed in the infinite goodness of God) are going in exactly the wrong direction. Instead, what would happen if we read this passage as a protest against God, or against a particular notion of God (hierarchical, authoritarian, *male*) or against a particular group that represented that theological perspective (perhaps sages or priests)?

I made an assumption earlier in this chapter which I must now discuss and justify. I associated the Israelite god, YHWH, with the deaths of those children. Now we must consider that and some other possible explanations for the troubling events of this story. At first glance, deity is barely present, if at all, in the plot. God never appears either by speaking or in a vision. No divine name is evoked except in Elisha's curse ("He cursed them, evoking the magical name of YHWH"—my translation). Many have examined the story anthropologically, regarding it (correctly) as a typical shamanic story. It has been compared to stories of shamans in Tibet, in Mexico, and among other oral and semi-oral cultures. In these stories, the shaman employs magic through the force of her or his personality or exertion of will to shape events. If the story of Elisha and the children can be reduced to an argument that "this shaman is very powerful and not to be trifled with," then the theological problem can be eliminated.

There are, however, two distinct places within the narrative where one discovers God, and the encounter alienates us from our comfortable theological perspectives. The first, of course, is the prophet Elisha. Although one would assume that such a man would be designated by some theophoric title, such as "prophet of YHWH," or "Man of God," the narrator usually refers to him by his personal name. The covenantal god of Israel appears most suddenly and violently in this story in Elisha's curse formula. And even here, it appears as little more than a magical incantation to empower the curse and make it effective. However, this little curse is the link between the words of the prophet and the horrific results, the mauling of the children. It was not Elisha's own words, but words he spoke "in YHWH's name," that had the required effect. We must, therefore, conclude in this story that either YHWH is an inanimate force that any skillful practitioner of magic might control[10] or YHWH, in some way, lent his approval and support to

Elisha's rage, and was so angry himself that he had the offending children killed, horribly. A different, less likely possibility, would assert that YHWH gave power to Elisha when the prophet was commissioned (2 Kings 2), and YHWH could not take it back or control how it was used because such gifts were irrevocable.

Complicity between Elisha and YHWH to accomplish the prophet's revenge on the youngsters is most consistent with a theme I have been tracing through this book, that God is dangerous and unpredictable, and might likely act in a jealous, selfish, petulant, bitter, vengeful, and spiteful way. Might not the vanity of the prophet somehow correspond to YHWH's vanity?

This is the place that YHWH appears—not in the curse, which is a mere formula, but rather in the person and power of the prophet who acts in God's stead, on God's behalf in meting out punishment for disrespect of the divine majesty. In this case, YHWH's majesty links to the prophet's self-consciousness. He is self-conscious because he was bald. What kind of god kills children because they show disrespect to his prophet? God appears to be petty, selfish, vain, and easily angered, and overreacts in judgment and frequently regrets his actions.

So, if in the economy of the passage, an insult to the prophet is an insult to YHWH who stands behind the prophet, then the way that a prophet reacts to such slights is the way that God reacts, and therefore one must be especially careful not to slight YHWH. Or it can be said that YHWH vehemently defends his prophets as if he were defending himself. And that defense is swift and ruthless, without mercy.

But, since the actual raw, physical strength within the story rests with the bears and not the prophet, one can examine the role of the bears for traces of divine activity, as well. They "came up out of the woods," a place that was dark and frightening. So out from this uncreated place, apart from the realm of human control and civilization, come two wild animals, bringing their chaos and violence into the human realm. This takes place on the borderland between the wild and the tame.

This story locates divine activity in this borderland. The punishment comes not from the physical hand of the prophet, or from the human community, but from the place of wildness, the wilderness. In the story then, the wildness manifests the divine. YHWH ripped apart the children, the bears working on his behalf, representing him. Might we then make the connection that YHWH is like the bears, or that the bears equal YHWH?

This archetypal reading of the bears must be nuanced by a reading informed by issues of gender. This passage also contains the rigid, authoritarian structure of patriarchal society, in which an older, male figure catches an insult—and hair is intimately connected with male virility and power in the Bible.[11] In contrast to that ordered maleness, the bears are female. They express mindless violence, willing to tear apart the orderly world of the children and of their parents. Some suggest that the bears' anger results from the mothers being separated from their cubs. Just so, divine power is often associated with the destructive forces of nature—storm, wind, fire, thunder and lightning, rain, earthquakes, and volcanoes. The emphasis on the gender of the bears could either function as a naturalistic explanation for the bears' aggressive approach to the boys, or it could be an attempt to place a feminine face upon divine wrath perceived in natural disaster.[12]

Whether God's presence is mediated through the curse, or through the prophet, or the bears, God is that which threatens the human community by rigidly retaliating against any perceived slight. God is the force that comes hurtling down upon the community with the destructive force of an earthquake, by slavering, murderous animals. Such a god is dangerous, to be approached (if at all) with great caution and servile fear. The curse, the man, and the bears encompass the single divine act, the retribution for the slight, death by animals tearing.

Such a god is neither protective, nor nurturing, nor positive in any way.

A town that had suddenly lost its children in a violent sense-less act of nature would very likely regard deity as a blind, de-structive force, and blame the divine's human representative, which in this case is the bitter and judgmental face of the vain prophet. The people would blame Elisha for failing to protect the children, and even blame God for turning against them him-self. Ultimately, the two violent images, the condemning judge and the marauding she-bears, begin to blend into one horrific, frightening image of violence, threat, and senseless activity.

There is however one more image within the story, the boys. They are young, disrespectful of grownup authority, playful, rebellious, and free. In a way they participate in both worlds, that of human culture (they are the future inheritors of the so-cial world) and the world of the woods, because they are wild and unrestrained. Whereas the bears stand for chaos, danger-ous in the extreme, do the chaotic boys represent such a dan-ger? They are a danger to the prophet, who has the bears do his dirty work because he feared the youngsters' lack of decorum, which would break in and threaten his superior position. Sim-ilarly, YHWH cast the first man and first woman out of the gar-den lest they threaten *his* superiority.

So, considering the negative portrayal of the prophet in this narrative, might we read back into the mockery of the boys a *positive* reaction to the bitter and violent religiosity of the new prophet?[13] Perhaps the mockery of the children pokes into Eli-sha's religious pretensions, and by extension, also attacks the pretensions of other structures of authority. In that case, the children's mockery is also a faithful response and meant to give hope to a dreary passage. Their death at the hands of the very chaos they sought to evoke becomes a kind of literary martyr-dom (I am not suggesting that children should be martyrs to anything in the real world), martyrdom to the dissenter, the outsider, the one who attacks unjust power.

And as I suggested earlier, the community, whatever community that might be, that suffers violence at the hands of nature, or at the hands of unjust human authority, might embrace the belief in the kind of god portrayed in the Elisha story. Although not exactly worshiping such a god, they would fight with deity in these stories, and through these stories, agonize over God's unfairness, the bitterness of such a world. And that is a kind of worship. Perhaps such a community produced this tale, and perhaps similarly constituted communities might need to start telling these stories again, stories of the dangerous God.

Conclusion

"He can't help us very much," Barney said. "Some, maybe. But he stands with empty, open hands; he understands he wants to help. He tries, but . . . it's just not that simple. Don't ask me why. Maybe even he doesn't know. Maybe it puzzles him too. Even after all the time he's had to mull over it . . .

Anne said, "But I know you're wrong, Barney. Something which stands with empty, open hands is not God. It's a creature fashioned by something higher than itself, as we were. God wasn't fashioned and He isn't puzzled.

Philip K. Dick, The Three Stigmata of Palmer Eldritch

"Did he who made the lamb make thee?" In the Blake poem, the Tyger is not exactly hostile in the usual sense, just frightening in its strength and raw power, such as we see in Leviathan and Rahab, the mythical chaos monsters found in some ancient Near Eastern literature, including the Hebrew Bible. On the assumption that what God makes somehow reflects the divine character, what does the Tyger tell us about God? That is what I have been addressing for the past six chapters. Each successive passage seems to raise the same question: "What kind of a god do we have here?" Or to repeat the sentence I give to my classes, "If all you knew about God came from this passage, how would you describe the divine being?" That is one question. The other that arises most frequently is, "What kind of

people, what kind of a religion might we find, where people believe in such a god?

Thomas Thompson, a historian of the ancient Near East, believes that the ancient Israelites never imagined that their god,
whom Thompson calls "Elohei shamayim," was anything like
these stories they told.[1] One must then ask, Why did they tell
such stories? They were certainly not connected with any god
other than YHWH in the minds of the readers. Ancient Israelites
didn't read these stories and say, this must be about some other
god. Rather, these stories served some function for them. That
function was in various cases complex. For instance, these stories might have been a source of entertainment. Or they might
have functioned for them in the political realm, as a means to
gain, maintain, or undermine the structures of power in their society. But on many levels, the stories must have functioned theologically; the stories communicated the Israelites' imaginative
constructions of God—they told the people what they themselves believed God was like. This must be taken into account regardless of how troubling these passages are to us. These stories,
since they were about God, must have scratched some theological itch they had. I cannot imagine their telling otherwise.

The entertainment value of these stories is obvious. They
strike a chord in nearly everyone who hears them. They also
generate enormous scholarly activity. Invariably, these stories
have provoked in class discussion and papers, the most personal and enthusiastic reactions. But they are also stories of
deep cultural memory. They carry important information from
earlier generations to our own time—messages ancient people
took seriously enough to copy and preserve laboriously over
many centuries. We cannot lightly dismiss them, although ultimately we may rebel against their portrayals. And we certainly
must not explain them away, do damage control and seek to
cover up their troubling elements through facile explanations.

Fredric Jameson, Marxist literary critic at Duke University, said, "Yet the disparate raw materials [that make up a literary text] are all clearly in one way or another social and historical: They come from someplace real. They bear, even cold, the traces of ancient struggles and of a once historical emergence."[2] Politically, I have suggested that these stories, by undermining the most basic theological verities (the goodness and reliability of God), undermine as well the structures of power within the society that tells them. I called these stories seditious because they suggested that things were not fair and orderly—that the cult was not a reliable way to protect oneself against God; neither was a pure heart. Awful things just happened, regardless of one's behavior. They depended on the erratic moods of an inconstant, often hostile, deity. So the strictures to obedience and submission to the divinely ordained authorities were all called into question. These would be ideal stories to be told by a group that wanted to overthrow a king or topple a political priesthood. However, we cannot know for sure that such groups are connected with these stories.

The theological ramifications of these stories are most interesting. Different ones will function at different times, sometimes within the same story, sometimes in relationship to other stories. In some sense, as I have suggested in certain chapters, the theological claim of a monster God addresses the questions of theodicy. How can there be evil and suffering in the world? Answer: because God causes it. God is not reliably "good" or "benevolent," in any human sense of the word. This provides an explanation for individual suffering in the world. I suggest that at many times it is desirable to have a god who is in control of everything, even if that necessitates a god who is not entirely trustworthy.

Certainly these stories suggest a kind of Promethean agnosticism: The following quotes might elucidate a bit of what I mean: "If this is what YHWH is like, I want nothing to do with him!" Or, "Because I can't imagine a god being like this, I can't imagine God at all." And gradually: "God can't possibly be like this. What other ways might God be?" And so, finally, ultimately, such stories become tremendously hopeful. What begins as Promethean rebellion might be transformed into a bold creative activity, akin to worship, but a kind of worship that embraces human dignity, encourages questions, and accepts the ambiguity that seems to permeate human experience.

We face a world in which we find terrible suffering and pain. We must process that pain or else we succumb to despair. Belief in a divine presence might help us deal with the reality of undeserved suffering and death, but might also make things worse. If there is a god, why does not that god do something? Is God powerless? Is God weak? I suggest that these narratives, which portray the venality of YHWH, might provide a structure for processing the evil in the world. There can be no one image of God that works in all circumstances. Perhaps the images projected in these stories can provide a positive source of theological information to make sense of our world. And this information leaves us the dire responsibility to make things better.

There is a cave
within the Mount of God, fast by his throne,
Where Light and Darkness in perpetual round
Graceful vicissitude, by day and night;
Light issues forth, and at the other door
Obsequious Darkness enters, till her hour
To veil the heaven, though darkness there might well
Seem twilight here.

John Milton, Paradise Lost

Gravity becomes frivolity that retains its memory of suffering
and continues its search for truth in the joy of perpetually
making a new beginning.

Julia Kristeva, The Kristeva Reader

NOTES

Introduction

1. This negative depiction might portray an essentially good god and present that god in a negative light, or perhaps depict a god who has a sinister side.

2. William Butler Yeats, "The Second Coming," in *Collected Poems* (London: MacMillan & Co., 1967), 210–11.

3. David Penchansky, *The Betrayal of God: Dissonance in Job* (Louisville, Ky.: Westminster/John Knox Press, 1989).

4. Henry Miller, *Tropic of Cancer* (New York: Grove Press, 1961), 2.

Chapter 1. YHWH the Monster: The *Insecure* God (Genesis 3)

This chapter, in an earlier form, was published in *The Monstrous and Unspeakable: The Bible as Fantastic Literature*, ed. George Aichele and Tina Pippin, 43–60 (Sheffield: Sheffield Academic Press, 1997).

1. Roger Schlobin, "Prototypic Horror: The Genre of the Book of Job," *Semeia* 60 (1992): 23–38, offered a definition of horror and the monstrous that has surprising affinities with the Garden of Eden narrative: "The three, critical elements of horror are (1) its distortion of cosmology (more specifically, in Job's case, theodicy); (2) its dark inversion of signs, symbols, processes and expectations that causes this aberrant world and (3) its monster-victim relationship with its archetypal devastation of individual will. . . . In general, the horror's creatures are blatantly oblivious to any human sense of order, ethics or morality. They are so evil that good is either unknown or has no impact on them. Their natures are incomprehensible to the epistemologies of their victims and monsters are completely capable of disintegrating their victims' bodies and souls" (24, 30).

2. "Good and evil" here means something like "from A to Z," "from coast to coast," the whole thing, covering the two extremes and everything in between. See John Dominic Crossan, "Felix Culpa and

Foenix Culprit: Comments of 'Direct and Third Person Discourse in the Narrative of the *Fall*' by Hugh C. White," *Semeia* 18 (1980): 110.

3. James Barr, *The Garden of Eden and the Hope of Immortality* (Minneapolis: Fortress Press, 1992), 5.

4. Walter Brueggeman, *Genesis* (Atlanta: John Knox Press, 1982), 45, offering a quintessential theological reading, argues that the character of the trees is ultimately unimportant to an understanding of the tale. I strongly disagree. The fact that there is no explanation for the trees is reason enough for Brueggeman to conclude that there is no narrative interest in the tree. I could just as easily conclude the exact opposite—that the *absence* of any explanation is an indication of how important the trees are, their origin and explanation being suppressed, creating natural interest/curiosity about their existence.

5. I added the words in italics to emphasize what I believe are the nuances of the Hebrew words *beyom* ("on the day") and *mut tamut* ("dying you shall die"). See Barr, *Garden*, 10: ". . . clearly, as an instant punishment. This kind of warning is a warning for *mortals*, and is well evidenced elsewhere in the Bible."

6. Barr, *Garden*, 57, explains this well: "How were the two trees related, the tree of knowledge and the tree of life? The text leaves us confused about this. In Genesis 2:9 it tells us that God made all sorts of trees to grow, 'and the tree of life in the midst of the garden and the tree of the knowledge of good and evil.' But in v. 17 the only tree that is forbidden is the tree of knowledge of good and evil, and nothing at all is said about the tree of life. In 3:3, when the woman is explaining to the snake which tree is forbidden, she defines it as 'the tree which is in the middle of the garden', and this is the only tree that is forbidden. That this was the tree of knowledge of good and evil follows naturally. . . . It now becomes important that they should not eat of the tree of life, which in fact has not been mentioned at all since the trees were first mentioned at 2:9. What is not clear is: why the tree of life was not forbidden as the tree of knowledge was; where it was in relation to the later tree; whether the humans had in fact been eating of the tree of life all along; and if they had not been eating of it, why they had not done so."

7. This prohibition was counterintuitive because the fruit was obviously beneficial to human well-being and advancement.

8. The story of the prodigal son (Luke 15:11–32) is a good example of this.

9. I considered briefly whether in fact there was death in the fruit,

and YHWH/Elohim was warning the humans of the danger of eating it. There proved to be no danger in the fruit, however, and they did not die. It was not a warning of some danger outside of the danger of YHWH/Elohim himself. It was a threat. "If you do this I will punish you, and the punishment is that I shall kill you." That only YHWH/Elohim links the consumption of the fruit with death, that the *name* of the tree indicates the only inevitable consequence (the acquisition of knowledge), and that they did not die are indications that the death was an intended and willed punishment, and not an inevitable consequence.

10. Brueggeman, *Genesis*, 47, regards the serpent as of no independent significance to the progression of the story. He says: "The serpent is a device to introduce the new agenda. The serpent has been excessively interpreted. Whatever the serpent may have meant in earlier versions of the story, in the present narrative it has no independent significance. . . . It is not a phallic symbol or Satan or a principle of evil or death."

11. Umberto Cassuto, *A Commentary on the Book of Genesis* (Jerusalem: Magnes Press, 1961), 140–42, notes that, "According to ancient Talmudic sources, the primeval serpent is just a species of animal, although differing in character from the serpent of today, and resembling man in his upright stature and in his manner of eating . . . it is beyond doubt that the Bible refers to an ordinary, natural creature, for it is distinctly stated here: BEYOND ANY BEAST OF THE FIELD *that the Lord God had made*." He goes on to note that this interpretation has some difficulties, particularly in that the serpent *spoke* and that it had hidden *knowledge*.

12. The woman had said, "We may eat of the fruit of the trees in the garden; but God said, 'You shall not eat of the fruit of the tree that is in the middle of the garden, nor shall you touch it, or you shall die' " (Gen. 3:2, 3).

13. "The serpent tricked me, and I ate" (Gen. 3:13). The word "tricked," interestingly enough, is frequently used of a god or supernatural being deceiving humans (i.e., 2 Kings 19:10: "Let not the god whom you trust deceive you"). Note that many ancient cultures have "trickster" gods.

14. Admittedly, it may be argued successfully that those are all rhetorical questions, spoken by one who already knows the answers, as clearly YHWH knows the answer to the question he asks Cain, "Where is your brother?" (Gen. 4:9). In that narrative, YHWH's next comment indicates he knows exactly where the brother is: "Your

brother's blood cries out to me from the ground." In this case (Genesis 2–3), however, there is no reliable grammatical or contextual way to demonstrate that YHWH/Elohim knew the answers to these questions (but cf. Cassuto, *Genesis*, 155–58, for the argument that these are strictly rhetorical questions).

15. For example, observe how Pamela Milne, "The Patriarchal Stamp of Scripture: The Implications of Structuralist Analyses for Feminist Hermeneutics," in *A Feminist Companion to Genesis*, ed. Athalya Brenner (Sheffield: Sheffield Academic Press, 1993), 162, exculpates deity: "The mythic theme of the fall has been used by the patriarchal mindset to posit that sexual differentiation, though bringing mutual joy, causes much complexity and pain. It has also been used to shift guilt or fault for the fall away from God (since the idea that God is ultimately responsible for evil is intolerable) and away from man (since it is no less intolerable for the male mindset that all the guilt should pass to man). It is the woman and the animals who assume the guilt in this myth."

16. James G. Williams, "A Response to Jobling: The Necessity of Being 'Outside,' " *Semeia* 18 (1980): 52, argues that YHWH/Elohim's motivation is mercy.

17. YHWH expressed similar sentiments in the Tower of Babel story: "Look, they are one people, and they have all one language; and this is only the beginning of what they will do; nothing that they propose to do will now be impossible for them" (Gen. 11:6). God acted not because of judgment, but rather to protect divine privilege.

18. Orson Scott Card, *Xenocide* (New York: Tor Books, 1989), 434.

19. David Jobling, "The Myth Semantics of Genesis 2:4b–3:24," *Semeia* 18 (1980): 41–49, constructs the tale in this manner: "The earth needs a skilled workman; but the only one available is stolen by a villain, who wishes to make selfish use of his services in his private garden. There is, however, a flaw in the villain's plan—if the man eats of a certain tree in the garden, the villain will lose his hold on him. But, by the agency of certain helpers, the man is brought to eat of the tree. When the villain discovers this, he *marks* both the man and the helpers (the curses). But he does not carry out the death sentence. Rather, he sends the man out of the garden, so that the original lack is liquidated . . . the main problem is with the character Yahweh. To characterize him as villain is not implausible, in view of 3:8 (the garden is for his own enjoyment) and v. 23 (where he feels "threatened" by the man!). As villain, he is the *opponent* of the main program . . . [but] Yahweh

stands out, indirectly but clearly, as *helper* of the main program. This role is by no means so overt as that of opponent, but it creates definite ambiguity" (42).

20. I interpret the death as a threat of punishment, and not an inevitable consequence.

21. Card, *Xenocide*, 434.

22. Barr, *Garden*, 14, makes some interesting comments in this regard: "The person who comes out of this story with a slightly shaky moral record is, of course, God. Why does he want to keep eternal life for himself and not let them share it? Even more seriously, why does he not want them to have knowledge of good and evil? What is wrong with this knowledge, that they should not possess it?" Cuthbert Simpson, "The Book of Genesis," in *The Interpreters Bible*, ed. G. A. Buttrick (New York: Abingdon-Cokesbury Press, 1952), 1:501, observes regarding the serpent: "But the serpent, a demon hostile to God, told man the truth. He was thus no subtle tempter but, in intention at least, a benefactor of the human race. Man, thus enlightened, ate of the tree and became like God, knowing good and evil (v. 22). The potential threat to God's supremacy had thus become actual, so God, acting decisively and at once, drove him from the garden lest he should put forth his hand and take also of the tree of life, and eat (v. 22), and so make the threat permanent."

23. Cassuto, *Genesis*, 113 (among others) understands that the Tree of Knowledge imparts maturity, which is a mixed blessing. He says, "Out of fatherly love the Lord God forbade him to eat of the fruit, which would have opened before him the gateway to the knowledge of the world, the source of care and pain, and would have brought both his simplicity and his bliss to an end."

24. *The* Satan and Satan are to be distinguished. The first is a title (the loyal opposition) given to one of the angelic figures in the book of Job. By the time the term becomes a name without the definite article, it represents a less ambiguous evil figure, more similar to Satan and the devil in the Christian Testament.

25. Roland Boer, *Jamesom and Jeroboam* (Atlanta: Scholars Press, 1996), 77.

26. "It is God who is placed in a rather ambiguous light. He has made an ethically arbitrary prohibition, and backed it up with a threat to kill which, in the event, he does nothing to carry out. He is of course angry, and the man and woman are frightened. But after issuing announcements of humiliations, limitations and frustrations to which

they will be liable, he goes on to care for them and provide the necessary clothes" Barr, *Garden*, 12.

27. Gordon J. Wenham, *Genesis 1–15*, Word Biblical Commentary (Waco, Tex.: Word Books, 1987), provides a good example of a theological reading. See esp. 63–64, 73.

28. "What God 'knows' which he has not told man is that eating of the forbidden tree will make man 'like God, knowing good and evil' (v. 6). The prohibition thus is made to appear not in the interest of humans, but only of the deity. This deceptive discrepancy between what 'God knows' and what he says is designed to dissolve the illocutionary force of the prohibition." (Hugh C. White, "Direct and Third Person Discourse in the Narrative of the 'Fall.'" *Semeia* 18 (1980):92–106. For a discussion of the fruit as bringing "mature knowledge," see Lyn M. Betchel, "Rethinking the Interpretation of Genesis 2:4b–3:24," in *A Feminist Companion to Genesis*, ed. Athalya Brenner (Sheffield: Sheffield Academic Press, 1993), 88.

29. Graham Greene, *The Honorary Consul* (London: Penguin Books, 1973), 224–26.

Chapter 2. Uzzah, YHWH's Friend:
The *Irrational* God (2 Samuel 6)

1. I am here conflating two disparate passages, 1 Samuel 6 and 2 Samuel 6, which have much in common, but some significant differences.

2. This is the standard, Wellhausian reconstruction of the political structure of ancient Israel. See George B. Caird, "The First and Second Books of Samuel: Introduction and Exegesis," in *The Interpreter's Bible*, ed. George Arthur Buttrick (New York: Abingdon-Cokesbury Press, 1953), 1076. A. A. Anderson, *2 Samuel*, Word Biblical Commentary (Dallas: Word Books, 1989), 100, notes that David moves the ark to Jerusalem in an effort to provide legitimization for his dynasty and royal city. See also Walter Brueggemann, *Genesis* (Atlanta: John Knox Press, 1990), 247–48. He notes that David moves the ark to Jerusalem in an effort to provide legitimization for his dynasty and royal city. "The outcome is that Jerusalem, recently acquired from the Canaanites, is now authorized as the seat of Israel's precious tradition, the locus of YHWH's presence, and the place of appeal to YHWH in time of need (cf. 1 Kings 8:31–54) . . . the reclaiming of the ark is an opportunity for a powerful propagandistic effort to assert the new regime

as the rightful successor to the old tribal arrangement." See also Ronald E. Clements, *God and Temple: The Idea of the Divine Presence in Ancient Israel* (Oxford: Basil Blackwell Publisher, 1965), 412–42, who states: "By this act David brought over the old traditions of the amphictyony to his new capital, and established it beyond any question as the chief sanctuary of YHWH."

3. The following is a more complete list of theoretical explanations for Uzzah's demise: (a) he did not recognize that in Nacon's threshing floor they had entered a sacred space; (b) he touched the ark—he was not an appropriate person to touch the ark; (c) Uzzah was simply subject to the erratic and dangerous will of God.

4. Anderson, *2 Samuel,* 103; Peter Ackroyd, *The Second Book of Samuel* (Cambridge: Cambridge University Press, 1977), 66.

5. Henry Preserved Smith, *A Critical and Exegetical Commentary on the Books of Samuel,* International Critical Commentary (Edinburgh: T. & T. Clark, 1977), 294, asserts that "there is no Hebrew word *sl* known to us: [various versions] seem to go back to a common source which interpreted the word by the Aramaic. The present tendency is to regard the phrase as the mutilated remains of the words of the Chronicler: "because he had stretched his hand against the ark . . ."

6. The assumption that the object of the verb "stretch forth" is "Uzzah's hand" is not as big an assumption as some of the others, because of the verb that follows: "to grasp." Grasping implies the use of the hands.

7. YHWH killed him because of his *hsl* (this phrase does not occur in the LXX), but since we do not know what *hsl* means, that does not help us.

8. See Leviticus 10.

9. Other examples are Leviticus 10: Nadab and Abihu died "before the LORD"; 1 Samuel 15:33: Samuel hewed Agag to pieces "before the LORD."

10. I do not mean to imply that 2 Samuel 6 and Psalm 24 were written by the same person, or even at the same time—merely that they both seem to refer to the sacred ark entering Jerusalem.

11. The Vulgate and a manuscript of the LXX leave out this last phrase, which suggests that it is dittography.

12. The description the ark, v. 2, ". . . called by the name of the LORD of hosts." Caird, "Books of Samuel," 1077: "Arnold has put forward a most ingenious theory to account for the reading of the MT. He suggests that the original reading was 'over which had been called the name of

the Lord of hosts'; when the name YHWH was no longer pronounced in public worship a scribe wrote above the line as a substitute to be used by readers 'the name of him who is enthroned upon the cherubim' and the words of the gloss slipped into the text." That is almost my theory, but I would say that the second *hashem* is meant to substitute for YHWH (same as Arnold) but simply replaced it sloppily; "name of YHWH" becomes "name of the name." It is certainly an odd construction, but we cannot rule out the possibility that *shem-shem* might have some previously unknown technical meaning, some way to intensify the connection between YHWH's name and the ark, something like, "The name, indeed the name." Anderson, *2 Samuel*, 98, suggests dittography.

13. In the second procession 2 Samuel only refers to "those who bore it," with no reference to means of conveyance or the individuals who carried it, priests or not, Levites or not.

14. The addition of sacrifice, of David dancing, for instance.

15. The passage as a whole strongly supports the Jerusalem cult, the only ones who seem able to properly handle the ark.

16. In a later effort, in Chronicles (1 Chron. 16:5), even Obed-edom is listed among the Levites, and thus the poor man loses his distinct tribal identity as a Philistine and becomes absorbed in the Levitical tradition.

17. Smith, *Samuel*, 292–93, seems to think this is explicit. He calls it "a palpable violation . . ." The Kohathites thus became stand-ins for the Nadabites (from Aaron's son, Nadab?).

18. Might it be fair to assume that the priest-conveyance was the preferred way of the Zadokites in Jerusalem, who had just joined in alliance with David and needed to be catered to? There is no significance to the modes of transportation, no intrinsic superiority in priests' backs over the shoulders of oxen. So the preference for "priests-of-burden" must have a political basis.

19. This interpretation appears to come from a group desiring to elevate the Jerusalemite priesthood. This argument would most likely be framed in the second Temple period, which is the time usually associated with the Chronicler. These stories I have offered, though different from each other in emphasis, are not opposites, or in any way mutually exclusive.

20. It is impossible to translate this line ("burst forth with an outburst") and in any way make it sound smooth in English. It has the sense of the infinitive absolute (as in "Dying you shall die/you shall surely die," Gen. 2:17).

21. Job, Jeremiah, Habakkuk, Moses, Abraham, are some notable examples.

22. These two emotions might indicate two sources, one in which David reacted with fear and the other with anger. But the juxtaposition of the two emotions creates an interesting tension.

23. The first reading might also be regarded as a *backreading*—I am reading "back" into 2 Samuel my own imposed, imaginary understanding.

Chapter 3. The Fatal Census:
The *Vindictive* God (2 Samuel 24)

1. Some have noted the word "again" (*vayosef*) as linking the passage with 2 Samuel 21, which is the only other place in the David narratives where YHWH is spoken of as being angry with Israel, and there coincidentally the Israelites suffer three years of famine, which was one of the choices given to David in chapter 24. Note also the Midrash (tracing the anger of YHWH to Saul's failure to slaughter the Amalekite King Agag): To what else can the words "And again the anger of the Lord was kindled against Israel? And just what happened then to cause the anger of God to be kindled again against Israel?" (*Pesikta Rabbati*, trans. William G. Braude [New Haven, Conn.: Yale University Press, 1968], 203). The tale continues, when during the count, the men came to the place where Uriah the Hittite should be counted, it made YHWH angry all over again.

2. See below for a discussion of census as sin.

3. From the Talmud, *Seder Zera'im* (London: Soncino Press, 1948): In commenting on an earlier use of the word *sut* in 1 Sam. 26:19), "'If it be the Lord that hath stirred thee up against me, let Him accept an offering.' R. Eleazar said: Said the Holy One blessed be He, to David: Thou callest me a 'stirrer-up'. Behold, I will make thee stumble over a thing which even school-children know, namely, that which is written, 'When thou takest the sum of the children of Israel according to their number, then shall they give every man a ransom for his soul unto the Lord . . . that there be no plague among them . . . '" They suggest that because in an earlier conversation he suggests that the Lord had stirred Saul up. Well, now the Lord would show David what it was like to be stirred up.

4. Jon Levenson, *Creation and the Persistence of Evil* (San Francisco: Harper & Row, 1988), 44, speaks of rabbinic liturgy that changes the

text of Isaiah, "changes God's boast that he 'make peace and create evil' into the evasive affirmation that he 'makes peace and creates everything.'"

5. "[The rabbis] maintained that the king's tongue was not free from taint. David, in his entreaty with Saul, says, "If it be the Lord that hath stirred thee up against me, let Him accept an offering (1 Sam. 26:19). The rabbis consider this an unbecoming allusion to God, and in their opinion, David came to grief because of it in the matter of the census. Israel Moses Ta-Shma, "David in the Aggada," *Encyclopaedia Judaica* (Jerusalem: Keter Pub., 1972), 5:1328–29.

6. See above for discussion of ultimately unsuccessful efforts to link this passage with 2 Samuel 21.

7. It is not totally clear, but likely, that this tribunal is in fact also God. Frequently God appears as both witness, prosecuting and defense attorney, judge, and jury.

8. I am grateful to Shoshana Brown for this and the other rabbinic references.

9. In 1 Sam. 10:8 Samuel commands Saul to wait for him at Gilgal, to offer the sacrifice. However, there was no command from YHWH. Samuel's estimation of his own authority seems inappropriately large.

10. Scholars have accused David of a lack of faith because of his use of strategy, that is, by ascertaining his strength and not depending on YHWH. However, not every king who used strategy was condemned for lack of faith! Joshua was depicted as a brilliant strategist, as was David in other contexts.

11. The issue is not nearly as cut-and-dried as I present it here. See Thomas L. Thompson's "A New Attempt to Date the Patriarchal Narratives," *Journal of the American Oriental Society* 68 (1978): 76–84, for a discussion of the complexities of determining the relationship between textual doublets within the Hebrew Bible. We cannot be truly certain, from a historical perspective, that the writing in 2 Samuel preceded the writing in 1 Chronicles. It appears a likely reconstruction, but its temporal position does not affect my thesis.

12. Edward Lewis Curtis and Albert Alonzo Madsen, *A Critical and Exegetical Commentary on the Books of Chronicles* (Edinburgh: T. & T. Clark, 1910), 245–46, offer the following position regarding the ways Chronicles differs from 2 Samuel: (1) Satan instead of Yahweh is the instigator of the census. (2) The officers of the army, there associated with Joab, are omitted, and also the description of the country

traversed and the time occupied in taking the census. (3) The results of the census differ. (4) According to Chronicles, no count of Levi and Benjamin was made, while according to 2 Samuel, all the tribes appear to have been counted. (5) In Chronicles, David sees the destroying angel "between earth and heaven," while in 2 Samuel he is simply described as "by the threshing floor." (6) In Chronicles, the elders appear with David, and both are clothed with sackcloth and fall prostrate. This description is wanting in Samuel. (7) Chronicles also adds Ornan, who upon seeing the angel went into hiding with his four sons. (8) The price paid for the threshing floor varies. (9) The fire from heaven is not mentioned in 2 Samuel. (10) 1 Chronicles 21:26 and 1 Chronicles 22:1 are wanting in 2 Samuel.

13. Levenson, *Creation*, 44, writes regarding the Chronicles story, "[Note] the Chronicler's handling of David's catastrophic decision to take a census of Israel and Judah. Whereas 2 Samuel 24:1 says 'the anger of the Lord again flared up against Israel; and He incited David against them,' 1 Chronicles 21:1 tells us that 'Satan arose against Israel and incited David to number Israel.' Satan has replaced YHWH in the morally questionable role of instigator of sin and cause of destruction. A more refined and sophisticated sensibility has proven less able to tolerate the idea that God can be a cause of evil."

14. For instance, he murdered Uriah the Hittite (2 Sam. 11:15) and the Amalekite messenger who told him of Saul's death (2 Sam. 1:15).

15. The rabbis suggest that it was David's overweening self-confidence that led him to beg God to put him to the test with Bathsheba so that he could prove himself comparable in that respect to Abraham, Isaac, and Jacob (Sanh. 107a).

16. Some have claimed the choices indicate the "mercy of God," e. g., Peter Ackroyd, *The Second Book of Samuel* (Cambridge: Cambridge University Press, 1977), 232; Henry Preserved Smith, *A Critical and Exegetical Commentary on the Books of Samuel* (Edinburgh: T. & T. Clark, 1977), 391–92. But using the word *mercy* in such a way drains it of meaning.

17. Correspondence from Shoshana Brown: "There is a whole talmudic tractate of *fasts* undertaken in order to get God to send rain on the land. And the standard everyday liturgy includes a prayer for rain or dew. The precariousness of living off the land in Eretz Yisrael is a given. A drought (= famine) was not so unusual and people believed (*had* to believe, it seems) that God's 'mind' could be changed by prayer and fasting and a drought/famine ended. Perhaps they

thought a drought/famine was less a case of God's direct involvement and more a case of God's negligence."

18. Although, also included in that speech is this ascription to YHWH: "YHWH has said that he would dwell in thick darkness" (1 Kings 8:12).

Chapter 4. Nadab and Abihu, Martyrs:
The *Dangerous* God (Leviticus 10)

1. Richard Adams, *Shardik* (New York: Simon & Schuster, 1974), 398–99.

2. See Bernard J. Bamberger, *The Torah: A Modern Commentary* (New York: Union of American Hebrew Congregations, 1981), 800, and John C. H. Laughlin, "The 'Strange Fire' of Nadab and Abihu," *Journal of Biblical Literature* 95 (1976): 561.

3. Edward L. Greenstein, "Deconstruction and Biblical Narrative," *Prooftexts* 9 (1989): 64.

4. Robert Kirschner, "The Rabbinic and Philonic Exegesis of the Nadab and Abihu Incident (Lev. 10:1–6)," *Jewish Quarterly Review* 73 (1983): 389 [n. 36]. He continues: "However, an 'unknown Midrash' . . . to Num 11:11 classifies the incineration of Nadab and Abihu with six fatal fires: the fire that wrought havoc among the murmurers in the wilderness; the fire that consumed the company of Korah; the fire that destroyed Job's sheep; and the two fires that burned the first and second troops which Ahaziah sent against Elijah."

5. Bamburger, *Torah*, 804, says: "The cryptic narrative of the death of the two young men fairly cried for amplification by later preachers. Perhaps the Rabbis felt that the punishment was unduly harsh for a ritual infraction committed by inexperienced priests; yet they were sure God never acts unjustly. So they sought to solve the problem in various ways.

"Most often they expanded on the sinfulness of the young men. The prohibition of wine in verses 9ff. suggested that Nadab and Abihu had been drinking before they entered the sanctuary [20]. They were also guilty of arrogance and irreverence. From Exodus (24:9ff.), it was inferred that on Sinai Nadab and Abihu had gazed boldly at the Divine Presence—as if eating and drinking!—instead of turning their eyes humbly away, as Moses had done at the burning bush (Exod. 3:6). They had refused to marry and beget children because they deemed no woman good enough for me of their exalted birth. Yet despite their pride of ancestry, they had no respect for Moses and Aaron." See also David Damrosch, "Leviticus" in *The Literary Guide to the Bible*, ed. Robert Alter and Frank Kermode (Cambridge, Mass.: Harvard University Press, 1987), 70.

6. Greenstein, "Deconstruction," 63: "Explaining the death penalty of Nadab and Abihu appears to be the rabbis' most urgent exegetical necessity:—Even Titus, wicked as he was, could venture into the Holy of Holies, slash both veils, and go forth in peace. But Aaron's sons, who came into the Tabernacle to present an offering, were taken out burnt." See also Kirschner, "Rabbinic and Philonic Exegesis," 381.

7. This analysis will offer three kinds of context: (1) the wider immediate context: Aaron, Nadab, and Abihu and the dedication of the tent of meeting; (2) other examples of incense and instructions to priests regarding incense; (3) other incidents of "ritual misfire." I am indebted to Ronald L. Grimes, "Infelicitous Performances and Ritual Criticism," *Semeia* 41 (1988): 118, for the term "ritual misfire."

8. N. H. Snaith, *Leviticus and Numbers* (London: Thomas Nelson & Sons, 1967), 75–76.

9. Kirschner, "Rabbinic and Philonic Exegesis," 380: "MT, LXX and Targum Onqelos are silent about the motive(s) of Nadab and Abihu and the precise nature of their offense. Lev. 1:7 explicitly commands the sons of Aaron to put fire upon the altar; Lev. 8 describes how Aaron and his sons were duly consecrated as priests by Moses."

10. See also Lev. 1:5, 11; 2:2, 3, 10; 3:2, 5, 7; 6:14, 16, 20, 25; 7:31, 33, 34; 8:2, 6, 13, 14, 22, 24, 27, 31; 9:9, 12, 18.

11. See John C. H. Laughlin, "The 'Strange Fire' of Nadab and Abihu," *Journal of Biblical Literature* 95 (1976): 565; M. Haran, "The Uses of Incense in the Ancient Israelite Ritual," *Vetus Testamentum* 10 (1960): 115 [n. 1].

12. Haran, "Incense," 118: "Wellhausen propounded the theory that, during most of the period of the First Temple, the use of incense was a characteristically idolatrous form of worship which found its way into the cult of Jahweh only in the 7th Century BC."

13. Gnana Robinson, "The Prohibition of Strange Fire in Ancient Israel: A New Look at the Case of Gathering Wood and Kindling Fire on the Sabbath," *Vetus Testamentum* 28 (1978): 310, points to the following passages: Deut. 32:16; Jer. 2:25; Ezek. 16:32; Ps. 81:10; M. Sanhedrin 11:6; cf. Jer. 7:9, 18, 29:5. See also Baruch A. Levine, *The JPS Torah Commentary: Leviticus* (Philadelphia: Jewish Publication Society, 1989), 59.

14. Quoted in Nathaniel Micklem, "The Book of Leviticus," in *The*

Interpreter's Bible, ed. George Arthur Buttrick (New York: Abingdon-Cokesbury Press, 1953), 2:49–50.

15. Haran, "Incense," 115; see also Laughlin, "Strange Fire," 561: "Here too, this offering in itself is completely acceptable to P as a genuine ritual act; indeed, it is precisely because the act is ritually legitimate that it can serve as a *test* of the fitness of Korah and his company to officiate as priests. While those participating in the rebellion are not charged with the offense of offering "strange fire" to YHWH, it seems more than coincidental that they suffer the same fate as Nadab and Abihu (cf. v. 36)."

16. There is no effective way to connect the two sources, the deuteronomistic source of 1 Kings 13 and the priestly source of Exodus 30 and Numbers 16. Haran's insistence ("Incense," 126, 128, 129) that the offense in all these cases is inappropriate incense is not persuasive. He disputes (correctly in my opinion) Julius Wellhausen's claim that in ancient Israel offerings of incense are always related to offerings to strange gods (123–24).

17. 2 Chronicles 26:16–21; see Snaith, *Leviticus and Numbers,* 75, for a discussion of this passage.

18. See Haran, "Incense," 114–15.

19. Grimes, "Infelicitous Performances," 107, discusses "misfires" and "abuses."

20. Grimes, "Infelicitous Performances," 118.

21. Greenstein, "Deconstruction," 62

22. Kirschner , "Exegesis," 382, lists the various accusations pinned upon the two men: (1) Nadab and Abihu presumed to decide the law in the presence of Moses. (2) They approached too close to the divine presence. (3) They brought an improper offering. (4) They brought strange fire from an oven. (5) They neglected to consult first with one another (or with Moses). (6) They drank wine before approaching the altar. (7) They approached with unwashed hands and feet. (8) They lacked the prescribed number of garments (i.e., the robe). (9) They fathered no children (cf. Num. 3:4). (10) They were arrogant: (a) they thought no women to be worthy of their status; (b) they longed to replace Moses and Aaron. (11) They gazed greedily upon the divine presence (cf. Ex. 24:9–11).

23. John E. Hartley, *Leviticus,* Word Biblical Commentary (Dallas: Word Books, 1992), 131.

24. Kirschner, "Exegesis," 382–83, offers two *positive* reasons for the death: (1) They concluded that fire was necessary because the di-

vine presence, *skynh*, had been withheld from Israel. God said to them, "I shall honor you more than you have honored Me; you brought Me impure fire, but I will burn you with pure fire. (2) "Upon beholding the fire of divine approval immediately preceding their action (Lev. 9:23–24) they joyfully arose 'to add love to love.' Finally, they are considered to have suffered the death of the righteous."

25. Greenstein, "Deconstruction," 60. See also Kirschner, "Exegesis," 390, who notes, "The catalogue of Rabbinic accusations—presumption, carelessness, drunkenness, pride, celibacy, arrogance, etc.—tries to refute a difficulty that does not exist for Philo: why God would inflict death upon Aaron's sons . . . he averts the problem of theodicy."

26. Robinson, "Prohibition," 309.

27. Could the priestly writer have been alluding to two other pairs of brothers who didn't do well in the priestly ministry, the two sons of Eli—Hophni and Phineas? Or to the two sons of Samuel—Joel and Abijah? The sons of Eli were killed in battle against the Philistines. The sons of Samuel suffered no violent end, but suffered in obscurity, by the loss of their ministry. But Nadab and Abihu—earlier in the time line of biblical narrative, but written about after these others—must be judged according to more complex standards.

28. Haran, "Incense," 129.

29. The "strange fire" of Nadab and Abihu can be defined, then, as a fire "kindled by ordinary, human means or at least taken from some human, profane source." See Laughlin, "Strange Fire," 561.

30. Greenstein, "Deconstruction," 61.

31. Hartley, *Leviticus,* 130; Peretz Segal, "The Divine Verdict of Leviticus X 3," *Vetus Testamentum* 29 (1984): 94.

32: Greenstein, "Deconstruction," 57.

33. Segal, "Divine Verdict," 92.

34. Levine, *Leviticus,* 60.

35. Bamberger, *Torah,* 801.

36. Hartley, *Leviticus,* 134.

37. Bamberger, *Torah,* 803, offers this paraphrase: *"And such things have befallen me!* Clearly I am not in favor with God at present. For me to eat sin offering, implying that my intercession had won forgiveness for the people would be unsuitable."

38. Note the translation in Bamberger, *Torah,* 803: "And when Moses heard this, he approved."

39. Greenstein, "Deconstruction," 63.

40. Some in later religious traditions blame it on a devil and thus

diminish the power of God, or see it as something beyond the discourse about God, pointing to the fates, who are older than the gods and don't follow any of the rules, something from an altogether different realm.

Chapter 5. The Bloody Bridegroom:
The *Malevolent* God (Exodus 4:24–26)

1. The term "feet" is likely a circumlocution or euphemism for the genitals. See Isaiah 6:2; Ruth 3:4–14.

2. See Julian Morgenstern, "The 'Bloody Husband' (?) (Exod. 4:24–26) Once Again," *Hebrew Union College Annual* 34 (1963): 45, 70.

3. Brevard Childs, *The Book of Exodus* (Philadelphia: Westminster Press, 1974), 103. Nahum M. Sarna, *The JPS Torah Commentary: Exodus* (Philadelphia: Jewish Publication Society, 1991), 26.

4. "In reference to" is the preferred translation of the Hebrew preposition *l*.

5. By "transmissional history," I mean the process by which in the ancient world a text would be copied, edited, collected, expanded, rewritten, and suppressed, until the point where it reached relative fixity, where it could not be changed as drastically. At that point, the point of canonization in biblical literature, the activity shifts to conflicting interpretations, which are a different kind of rewriting.

6. Sarna, *Exodus*, 24; Umberto Cassuto, *A Commentary on the Book of Exodus*, trans. Israel Abrahams (Jerusalem: Magnes Press [English edition], 1967), 61; Moshe Greenberg, *Understanding Exodus* (New York: Behrman House, 1961), 121; all note the obscurities in the text.

7. Moreover, J. deGroot, "The Story of the Bloody Husband," *Old Testament Studies* 2 (1943): 14, notes an illuminating parallel to the redundancy of vv. 25–26. See also William H. Propp, "That Bloody Bridegroom," *Vetus Testamentum* 43 (1993): 497.

8. Cf. Childs, *Exodus*, 99, who discusses the redactional role of 26b.

9. Edgar J. Park, *The Book of Exodus*, in *The Interpreter's Bible*, ed. George Arthur Buttrick (New York: Abingdon Press, 1952), 1:882, speculates, "Probably included from a mass of similar discarded material because it seemed to the editor to give the origin of the rite of circumcision, it is of value to us in that it emphasizes the jungle of primitive superstitions out of which the religion of YHWH was developed."

10. Childs, *Exodus*, 100.

11. Childs, *Exodus*, 101.

12. Terence E. Fretheim, *Exodus* (Louisville, Ky.: Westminster/ John Knox Press, 1991), 78.

13. Sarna, *Exodus*, 25. See Cornelius Houtman, "Exodus 4:24–26 and Its Interpretation," *Journal of Northwest Semitic Languages* 11 (1983): 81–105, esp. 89.

14. Morgenstern, "Bloody Husband," 40.

15. Childs, *Exodus*, 96; Greenberg, *Understanding Exodus*, 110. See Donald E. Gowan, *Theology in Exodus: Biblical Theology in the Form of a Commentary* (Louisville, Ky.: Westminster John Knox Press, 1998), 34; William Dumbrell, "Exodus 4:24–26: A Textual Re-Examination," *Harvard Theological Review* 65 (1972): 285; Morgenstern, "Bloody Husband," 46.

16. Childs, *Exodus*, 96; Benno Jacob, *The Second Book of the Bible: Exodus* (Hoboken, N.J.: Ktav Publishing House, 1992), 106.

17. Propp, "Bloody Bridegroom," 495, notes that "Aquila has 'the God.' The paraphrase 'angel of the Lord' of the LXX and Targums Onqelos and Ps.-Jonathan is an attempt to mitigate the shock of the episode. Jub. xl 2 goes so far as to replace the Deity with Mastemah, the arch-fiend."

18. I avoid the use of the term or model "pre-critical" and "critical" or "modern" because of the very great philosophical and methodological questions such concepts raise. What I say here probably comes to the same thing.

19. Propp, "Bloody Bridegroom," 498, offers a good contrast between ancient and modern interpretations. See also Houtman, "Exodus 4:24–26," 93.

20. J. Coert Rylaarsdam, *The Book of Exodus*, in *The Interpreter's Bible*, ed. George Arthur Buttrick (New York: Abingdon-Cokesbury Press, 1952), 1:882.

21. Martin Noth, *Exodus: A Commentary*, trans. J. S. Bowden (Philadelphia: Westminster Press, 1962), 50.

22. Noth, *Exodus*, 49–50. For definitions of male circumcision, see Godfrey Ashby, "The Bloody Bridegroom: The Interpretation of Exodus 4:24–26," *Expository Times* 106 (1993): 203.

23. Propp, "Bloody Bridegroom," 509.

24. The story of Tobit, likely written much later, has an account of a "wedding demon" who murders bridegrooms on the couple's first night together, although there is no mention of circumcision as a

"warding-off" in that story. Rather the demon is driven away by the burning of a magical fish liver (Tobit 3:7–9; 6:14–18; 8:2–4).

25. Childs, *Exodus*, 97, referring to Wellhausen, notes: "the story was an attempt to explain how circumcision, which was originally a puberty rite, was transferred from adulthood to childhood in Israel. Accordingly, Moses had not been circumcised and was therefore attacked. Zipporah circumcised her son as a substitute and established a permanent change in the rite by its successful outcome. . . . the theory that the tradition functioned originally as an etiology remains a reconstruction which can be posited, but not demonstrated from the text itself."

26. Propp, "Bloody Bridegroom," 501–2.

27. Morgenstern, "Bloody Husband," 44.

28. Childs, *Exodus*, 97–98.

29. Hans Kosmala, "The 'Bloody Husband,'" *Vetus Testamentum* 12 (1962): 14–28. J. Philip Hyatt, *Commentary on Exodus* (London: Oliphants, 1971), 87.

30. Ronald E. Clements, *God and Temple* (Oxford: Basil Blackwell Publisher, 1965), 31–32.

31. Childs, *Exodus*, 97.

32. Childs, *Exodus*, 98; Greenberg, "Exodus," 115.

33. Morgenstern, "Bloody Husband," 48.

34. Marc Vervenne, *Studies in the Book of Exodus* (Louvain: University Press, 1996), 15; Propp, "Bloody Bridegroom," 501.

35. Morgenstern, "Bloody Husband," 67.

36. Morgenstern, "Bloody Husband," 42–43.

37. Propp, "Bloody Husband," 505.

38. Ibid., 511

39. Hyatt, *Exodus*, 87.

40. Sarna, *Exodus*, 25.

41. Propp, "Bloody Bridegroom," 499; Pamela Tamarkin Reis, "The Bridegroom of Blood: A New Reading (Exodus 4:24–26), *Judaism* 40 (1991): 324–36.

42. Ashby, "Bloody Bridegroom," 203.

43. This is a common story in many cultures, as Propp, "Bloody Bridegroom," 514, suggests.

44. Childs, *Exodus*, 100.

45. A similar fragmentary story retained for the editor's own purposes is found in Genesis 6 where the "divine beings" (*bene 'elohim*) have sexual relations with human women, and giants are born. It was

retained as a moral justification for YHWH's destroying the world by a flood.

46. Fretheim, *Exodus*, 78.

47. Whereas a significant consensus emerges about other things, such as the existence of the Yahwist document, or the multiple authorship of Isaiah.

48. Sarna, *Exodus*, 26: a stone knife is still widely preferred in primitive societies that practice circumcision.

49. Ibid., 25.

50. Ibid., 25: Perhaps Moses neglected this rite to avoid exposing a newly circumcised boy to the rigors of the journey. See Josh. 5:5, 7.

51. Noth, *Exodus*, 49.

Chapter 6. The Mad Prophet and the *Abusive* God (2 Kings 2:23–25)

1. John Gray, *I and II Kings: A Commentary* (Philadelphia: Westminster Press, 1970), 479.

2. Eric J. Ziolkowski, "The Bad Boys of Bethel: Origin and Development of a Sacrilegious Type," *History of Religions* 30 (1991):332–33.

3. C. F. Keil and F. Delitzsch, *Commentary on the Old Testament in Ten Volumes* (Grand Rapids: Wm. B. Eerdmans Publishing Co., 1980), 3:299–300.

4. Burke O. Long, *2 Kings* (Grand Rapids: Wm. B. Eerdmans Publishing Co., 1991), 34, has a more particular take on the primitive nature of the tale.

5. I am aware that "tribe" is a concept under significant attack in current anthropological thinking.

6. Alexander Rofé, "The Classification of the Prophetical Stories," *Journal of Biblical Literature* 89 (1970): 429–30.

7. Tamis Rentería, "The Elijah/Elisha Stories: A Socio-cultural Analysis of Prophets and People in Ninth-Century BCE Israel," in *Elijah and Elisha in Socioliterary Perspective* (Atlanta: Scholars Press, 1992), 76.

8. Gray, *I and II Kings*, 466.

9. Long, *2 Kings*, 104–5.

10. We see a different position on cursing in the story of Balaam, whom YHWH forbade to curse Israel, in spite of his obvious reputation as a skilled prophet and wielder of curses.

11. For example, Samson's hair, or David's men who were shamed when their beards were shaved.

12. I received this letter from a friend on the Internet, Sharron Manassa: "Do not forget to mention that the She-bear is a deity across the globe (Artemis, Ursa, the Bear-mother of some of the Native American tribes) and that such she-bears are usually depicted as mothering, or as helpers of women giving birth or suckling their babies. This inverts that protectiveness and proclaims to the people that their goddesses have turned against them and have become slaves of this new God."

13. In the chronology of 2 Kings 1–2, Elisha has just been appointed to replace Elijah, and has performed his first two miracles in this new office. Rather than an old, wizened figure, we have here a young man who must prove himself, and who has a difficult act to follow, his mentor Elijah.

Conclusion

1. Thomas L. Thompson, "How Yahweh Became God: Exodus 3 and 6 and the Heart of the Pentateuch," *Journal for the Study of the Old Testament* 68 (1995): 61–62.

2. Fredric Jameson, *The Seeds of Time* (New York: Columbia University Press, 1994), 168.

BIBLIOGRAPHY

Aberbach, M., and M. Smolar. "Aaron, Jeroboam and the Golden Calves." *Journal of Biblical Literature* 86 (1967): 139

Ackroyd, Peter R. *The Second Book of Samuel.* Cambridge: Cambridge University Press, 1977.

Adams, Richard. *Shardik.* New York: Simon & Schuster, 1974.

Anderson, A. A. *2 Samuel.* Word Biblical Commentary. Dallas: Word Books, 1989.

Ashby, Godfrey. "The Bloody Bridegroom: The Interpretation of Exodus 4:24–26." *Expository Times* 106:203–5.

Bamberger, Bernard J. *The Torah: A Modern Commentary.* New York: Union of American Hebrew Congregations, 1981.

Barr, James. *The Garden of Eden and the Hope of Immortality.* Minneapolis: Fortress Press, 1992.

Baumann, A. *"dmh,* II." In *Theological Dictionary of the Old Testament.* Grand Rapids: Wm. B. Eerdmans Publishing Co., 1975, 3:263–64.

Bechtel, Lyn M. "Rethinking the Interpretation of Genesis 2:4b–3:24." In *A Feminist Companion to Genesis,* edited by Athalya Brenner, 77–117. Sheffield: Sheffield Academic Press, 1993.

Bentzen, Aage. "The Cultic Use of the Story of the Ark in Samuel." *Journal of Biblical Literature* 67 (1948): 37–53.

Berquist, Jon L. "Postcolonialism, Imperial Ideologies, and the Formation of the Biblical Text." Postcolonialism Session of the Ideological Criticism Group, AAR/SBL Annual Meeting, 1996.

Berry, Wendell. "Pray without Ceasing." In *Fidelity.* New York: Pantheon Books, 1992.

Blenkinsopp, Joseph. "Kiriath-jearim and the Ark." *Journal of Biblical Literature* 88 (1969): 143–56.

Boer, Roland. *Jameson and Jeroboam.* Atlanta: Scholars Press, 1996.

Bowman, Richard G. "The Fortune of King David/The Fate of Queen Michal: A Literary Criticial Analysis of 2 Samuel 1–8. In *Telling Queen Michal's Story*, edited by David J. A. Clines and Tamara C. Eskenazi, 97–120. Sheffield: JSOT Press, 1991.

Brueggemann, Walter. *Genesis*. Atlanta: John Knox Press, 1982.

———. *First and Second Samuel*. Louisville, Ky.: Westminster/John Knox Press, 1990.

Caird, George B. "The First and Second Books of Samuel: Introduction and Exegesis." In *The Interpreter's Bible*, edited by George Arthur Buttrick. New York: Abingdon-Cokesbury Press, 1953.

Campbell, Antony F. *The Ark Narrative*. Missoula, Mont.: Scholars Press, 1975.

———. "YHWH and the Ark: A Case Study in Narrative." *Journal of Biblical Literature* 98 (1979): 31–43.

Card, Orson Scott. *Xenocide*. New York: Tor Books, 1989.

Carlson, R. A. "David and the Ark in 2 Samuel 6." In *History and Traditions of Early Israel*, edited by André LeMaire and Benedikt Otzen, 15–23. Leiden: E. J. Brill, 1993.

———. *David the Chosen King. A Traditio-Historical Approach to the Second Book of Samuel*. Uppsala: Almqvist and Wiksell, 1964.

Carroll, R. P. "The Elijah-Elisha Sagas: Some Remarks on Prophetic Succession in Ancient Israel." *Vetus Testamentum* 19 (1969): 400–15.

Cassuto, Umberto. *A Commentary on the Book of Genesis*. Part 1: From Adam to Noah. Translated by Israel Abrahams. Jerusalem: Magnes Press, 1961.

———. *A Commentary on the Book of Exodus*. Translated by Israel Abrahams. Jerusalem: Magnes Press, 1967.

Childs, Brevard S. *The Book of Exodus*. Old Testament Library. Philadelphia: Westminster Press, 1974.

Clements, Ronald E. *God and Temple, the Idea of the Divine Presence in Ancient Israel*. Oxford: Basil Blackwell Publisher, 1965.

———. *Exodus*. Cambridge: Cambridge University Press, 1972.

Clines, David J. A. "Punishment Stories in the Legends of the Prophets." In *Orientation by Disorientation: Studies in Literary Criticism and Biblical Literary Criticism*, edited by Richard A. Spencer, 167–83. Pittsburgh: Pickwick Press, 1980.

———. "Michal Observed: An Introduction to Reading Her Story." In *Telling Queen Michal's Story*, edited by David J. A. Clines and Tamara C. Eskenazi, 24–63. Sheffield: JSOT Press, 1991.

———. "Michal's Story in Its Sequential Unfolding." *In Telling Queen Michal's Story*, edited by David J. A. Clines and Tamara C. Eskenazi, 129–40. Sheffield: JSOT Press, 1991.

Cogan, Mordechai, and Hayim Tadmor. *II Kings: A New Translation with Introduction and Commentary.* Anchor Bible. New York: Doubleday & Co., 1988.

Crossan, John Dominic. "Felix Culpa and Foenix Culprit: Comments of 'Direct and Third Person Discourse in the Narrative of the *Fall*' by Hugh C. White." *Semeia* 18 (1980): 107–11.

Culley, R. *Studies in the Structure of Hebrew Narrative.* Philadelphia: Fortress Press, 1976.

Curtis, Edward Lewis, and Albert Alonzo Madsen. *A Critical and Exegetical Commentary on the Books of Chronicles.* Edinburgh: T & T. Clark, 1910.

Damrosch, David. "Leviticus." In *The Literary Guide to the Bible,* edited by Robert Alter and Frank Kermode, 66–77. Cambridge, Mass.: Harvard University Press, 1987.

Dumbrell, William. "Exodus 4:24–26: A Textual Re-Examination." *Harvard Theological Review* 65 (1972): 287–90.

Deist, F. "Two Miracle Stories in the Elijah and Elisha Cycles and the Function of Legend in Literature." In *Studies in Isaiah,* edited by W. C. van Wyk, 79–90. Pretoria: NHW Press, 1979/1980.

Dick, Philip K. *The Three Stigmata of Palmer Eldritch.* New York: Doubleday, 1965.

Ehle, Robert C. "The Grace of God." In *Telling Queen Michal's Story,* edited by David J. A. Clines and Tamara C. Eskenazi, 145–56. Sheffield: JSOT Press, 1991.

Eskenazi, Tamara C. "Michal in Hebrew Sources." In *Telling Queen Michal's Story,* edited by David J. A. Clines and Tamara C. Eskenazi, 157–74. Sheffield: JSOT Press, 1991.

Exum, J. C. "Murder They Wrote: Ideology and the Manipulation of Female Presence in Biblical Narrative." *USQR* 43 (1989): 19–39.

Fishbane, Michael. "Exodus 1–4: the Prologue to the Exodus Cycle." In *Exodus*, edited by Harold Bloom, 59–72. New York: Chelsea House Publishers, 1989.

Fohrer, G. *Die symbolischen Handlungen der Propheten.* 2d. ed. Zurich: Zwingli Verlag, 1968.

Fretheim, Terence E. *Exodus.* Interpretation. Louisville, Ky.: Westminster/John Knox Press, 1991.

Gaster, Theodore H. *Myth, Legend, and Custom in the Old Testament.* New York: Harper & Row, 1969.

Ginzberg, Louis. *The Legends of the Jews.* Philadelphia: Jewish Publication Society, 1946.

Gordon, Robert P. *I and II Samuel: A Commentary.* Grand Rapids: Zondervan, 1986.

Gowan, Donald E. *Theology in Exodus: Biblical Theology in the Form of a Commentary.* Louisville, Ky.: Westminster John Knox Press, 1994.

Gray, John. *I and II Kings: A Commentary.* 2d ed. Philadelphia: Westminster Press, 1970.

Greenberg, Moshe. *Understanding Exodus.* New York: Behrman House, 1969.

Greene, Graham. *The Honorary Consul.* London: Penguin Books, 1973.

Greenstein, Edward L. "Deconstruction and Biblical Narrative." *Prooftexts* 9 (1989): 43–71.

Grimes, Ronald L. "Infelicitous Performances and Ritual Criticism." *Semeia* 41 (1988): 103–22.

Haran, M. "The Uses of Incense in the Ancient Isrelite Ritual." *Vetus Testamentum* 10 (1960): 113–29.

Hartley, John E. *Leviticus.* Word Biblical Commentary. Dallas: Word Books, 1992.

Hecht, Richard. "Patterns of Exegesis in Philo's Interpretation of Leviticus." *Studia Philonica* 6 (1979–1980): 115.

Hill, Scott D. "The Local Hero in Palestine in Comparative Perspective." *In Elijah and Elisha in Socioliterary Perspective,* 37–74. Atlanta: Scholars Press, 1992.

Hobbs, T. R. "2 Kings 1 and 2: Their Unity and Purpose." *Studies in Religion/Sciences Religieuses* 13 (1984): 327–34.

————. *2 Kings.* Word Biblical Commentary. Waco, Tex: Word Books, 1985.

Hopkins, Gerard Manley. *Selected Poetry.* Oxford: Oxford University Press, 1996.

Houtman, Cornelius. "Exodus 4:24–26 and Its Interpretation." *Journal of Northwest Semitic Languages* 11 (1983): 81–105.

Hyatt, J. Philip. *Commentary on Exodus.* London: Oliphants, 1971.

Jacob, Benno. *The Second Book of the Bible: Exodus.* Translated by Walter Jacob. Hoboken, N.J.: KTAV, 1992.

Jameson, Fredric. *The Seeds of Time.* New York: Columbia University Press, 1994.

Jobling, David. "The Myth Semantics of Genesis 2:4b–3:24." *Semeia* 18 (1980): 41–49.

Keil, C. F., and F. Delitzsch. *Commentary on the Old Testament in Ten Volumes.* Vol. 3. Grand Rapids: Wm. B. Eerdmans Publishing Co., 1980.

Kirschner, Robert. "The Rabbinic and Philonic Exegesis of the Nadab and Abihu Incident (Lev. 10:1–6). *The Jewish Quarterly Review* 73 (1983): 375–93.

Kristeva, Julia. *The Kristeva Reader.* Edited by Toril Moi. New York: Columbia University Press, 1986.

Laughlin, John C. H. "'The 'Strange Fire' of Nadab and Abihu." *Journal of Biblical Literature* 95 (1976): 559–65.

Levenson, John. *Creation and the Persistence of Evil: The Jewish Drama of Divine Omnipotence.* San Francisco: Harper & Row, 1988.

Levine, Baruch A. *The JPS Torah Commentary: Leviticus.* Philadelphia: Jewish Publication Society, 1989.

————. "Leviticus, Book of." *Anchor Bible Dictionary,* edited by David Noel Freedman, 4: 311–21. New York: Doubleday, 1992.

Long, Burke O. "The Social Setting for Prophetic Miracle Stories." *Semeia* 3 (1975): 46–63.

————. *2 Kings.* The Forms of the Old Testament Literature, 10. Grand Rapids: Wm. B. Eerdmans Publishing Co., 1991.

Lundbom, J. R. "Elijah's Chariot Ride." *Journal of Jewish Studies* 24 (1973): 39–50.

Macalister, A. "Baldness." In *A Dictionary of the Bible,* edited by James Hastings. New York: Charles Scribner's Sons, 1898, 1: 234–35.

Macdonald, J. "The Status and Role of the Na'ar in Israelite Society," *Journal of Near Eastern Studies* 35 (1976): 147–70.

McCarter, Kyle P. "The Ritual Dedication of the City of David in 2 Samuel 6." In *The Word of the Lord Shall Go Forth,* edited by Carol L. Meyers and M. O'Connor, 273–78. Winona Lake, Ind.: Eisenbrauns, 1983.

Melville, Herman. *Moby Dick.* 1851. Reprint: Pleasantville, N.Y.: Reader's Digest Association, 1989.

Micklem, Nathaniel. *The Book of Leviticus.* In *The Interpreter's Bible,* edited by George Arthur Buttrick. New York: Abingdon-Cokesbury Press, 1953.

Miller, Henry. *Tropic of Cancer.* New York: Grove Press, 1961.

Miller, P. D., Jr., and J. J. M. Roberts. *The Hand of the Lord: A Reassessment of the "Ark Narrative" of 1 Samuel.* Baltimore/London: Johns Hopkins University Press, 1977.

Milne, Pamela J. "The Patriarchal Stamp of Scripture: The Implications of Structuralist Analyses for Feminist Hermeneutics." In *A Feminist Companion to Genesis,* edited by Athalya Brenner, 146–72. Sheffield: Sheffield Academic Press, 1993.

Montgomery, J. A., and H. S. Gehmann. *The Books of Kings.* 1896. International Critical Commentary. Edinburgh: T. & T. Clark, 1951.

Morgenstern, Julian. "On Leviticus 10,3." In *Oriental Studies Published in Commemoration of Paul Haupt,* edited by C. Adler and A. Ember, 97–102. Baltimore: Johns Hopkins Press, 1926.

———."The 'Bloody Husband' (?) (Exod. 4:24–26) Once Again." *Hebrew Union College Annual* 34 (1963): 35–70.

Nelson, Richard D. *First and Second Kings.* Atlanta: John Knox Press, 1987.

Newman, Murray. *The People of the Covenant.* Nashville: Abingdon Press, 1962.

Noth, Martin. *Exodus: A Commentary.* Translated by J. S. Bowden. Philadelphia: Westminster Press, 1962.

Overholt, Thomas W. "Seeing Is Believing: The Social Setting of

Prophetic Acts of Power." *Journal for the Study of the Old Testament* 23 (1982): 3–31.

Park, J. Edgar. *The Book of Exodus.* In *The Interpreter's Bible,* edited by George Arthur Buttrick. Nashville: Abingdon Press, 1952.

Pedersen, J. *Israel: Its Life and Culture.* London-Copenhagen: Oxford University Press, 1959.

Penchansky, David. *The Betrayal of God: Dissonance in Job.* Louisville, Ky.: Westminster/John Knox Press, 1989.

———. "God the Monster: Fantasy in the Garden of Eden." In *The Monstrous and the Unspeakable: The Bible as Fantastic Literature,* edited by George Aichele and Tina Pippin, 43–60. Sheffield: Sheffield Academic Press, 1997.

Pesikta Rabbati. Translated by William G. Braude. New Haven, Conn.: Yale University Press, 1968.

Plaskow, Judith. "Drawing the Awful Line between the Holy and the Profane." *Long Island Jewish World* (April 4–10, 1986).

Polak, F. "Theophany and Mediator: The Unfolding of a Theme in the Book of Exodus." In *Studies in the Book of Exodus: Redaction–Reception–Interpretation,* edited by Mark Vervenne, 113–47. Louvain: University Press, 1996.

Propp, William H. "That Bloody Bridegroom (Exodus IV 24–6)." *Vetus Testamentum* 43 (1993): 495–518.

Reis, Pamela Tamarkin. "The Bridegroom of Blood: A New Reading (Exodus 4:24–26). *Judaism* 40 (1991): 324–31.

Rentería, Tamis. "The Elijah/Elisha Stories: A Socio-cultural Analysis of Prophets and People in Ninth-Century B.C.E. Israel". In *Elijah and Elisha in Socioliterary Perspective,* 75–126. Atlanta: Scholars Press, 1992.

Robinson, Gnana. "The Prohibition of Strange Fire in Ancient Israel: A New Look at the Case of Gathering Wood and Kindling Fire on the Sabbath." *Vetus Testamentum* 28 (1978): 3.

———. *Let Us Be Like the Nations: A Commentary on the Books of 1 and 2 Samuel.* Grand Rapids: Wm. B. Eerdmans Publishing Co., 1993.

Robinson, J. *The Second Book of Kings.* Cambridge: Cambridge University Press, 1976.

Rofé, Alexander. "The Classification of the Prophetical Stories." *Journal of Biblical Literature* 89 (1970): 427–40.

Rylaarsdam, J. Coert. *The Book of Exodus.* In *The Interpreter's Bible,* edited by George Arthur Buttrick. New York: Abingdon-Cokesbury Press, 1952.

Sanda, A. *Die Bucher der Konige.* Exegetisches Handbuch zum Alten Testament. Munster: Aschendorffscher Verlag, 1911–12.

Sarna, Nahum M. "The Authority and Interpretation of Scripture in Jewish Tradition." In *Understanding Scripture: Explorations of Jewish and Christian Traditions of Interpretation,* edited by Clemens Thomas and Michael Wyschogrod, 9–20. New York: Paulist Press, 1987.

————. *The JPS Torah Commentary: Exodus.* Philadelphia: Jewish Publication Society, 1991.

Schlobin, Roger C. "Prototypic Horror: The Genre of the Book of Job." *Semeia* 60 (1992): 23–38.

Seder Zera'im. London: Soncino Press, 1948.

Segal, Peretz. "The Divine Verdict of Leviticus X 3." *Vetus Testamentum* 29 (1989): 91–95.

Shargent, Karla G. "Living on the Edge: The Liminality of Daughters in Genesis to 2 Samuel." In *A Feminist Companion to Samuel and Kings,* edited by Athalya Brenner. Sheffield: Sheffield Academic Press, 1994.

Simpson, Cuthbert A. *The Book of Genesis.* In *The Interpreter's Bible,* edited by George Arthur Buttrick. New York: Abingdon-Cokesbury Press, 1952.

Smith, Henry Preserved. *A Critical and Exegetical Commentary on the Books of Samuel.* 1898. Edinburgh: T. & T. Clark, 1977.

Snaith, N. H. *The First and Second Books of Kings: Introduction and Exegesis.* In *The Interpreter's Bible,* edited by George Arthur Buttrick. New York: Abingdon-Cokesbury Press, 1954.

————. *Leviticus and Numbers.* London: Thomas Nelson & Sons, 1967.

Sockman, Ralph W. *The First and Second Books of Kings: Exposition. The Interpreter's Bible,* edited by George Arthur Buttrick. New York: Abingdon-Cokesbury Press, 1954.

Stade, B., and Schwally F. Stade, with notes by P. Haupt. *The Books of Kings.* The Sacred Books of the Old Testament. Leipzig: J. C. Hinrichs, 1904.

Ta-Shma, Israel Moses. "David in the Aggada." In *Encyclopaedia Judaica*. Jerusalem: Keter Pub, 1972, 5: 1326–29.

Thompson, Thomas L. "How Yahweh Became God: Exodus 3 and 6 and the Heart of the Pentateuch." *Journal for the Study of the Old Testament* 68 (1995): 57–74.

———. "A New Attempt to Date the Patriarchal Narratives." *Journal of the American Oriental Society* (1978): 76–84.

Van der Toorn, Karel. "The Babylonian New Year Festival: New Insights from the Cunneiform Texts and Their Bearing on Old Testament Study." Vetus Testamentum Supplements 43 (1989): 331–44.

Van de Toorn, Karel, and Cees Houtman. "David and the Ark." *Journal of Biblical Literature* 113 (1994): 209–31.

Vervenne, Marc, ed. *Studies in the Book of Exodus: Redaction–Reception–Interpretation*. Louvain: University Press, 1996.

Wenham, Gordon J. *Genesis 1–15*. Word Biblical Commentary, Waco, Tex.: Word Books, 1987.

White, Hugh C. "Direct and Third Person Discourse in the Narrative of the 'Fall.'" *Semeia* 18 (1980): 92–106.

Williams, James G. "A Response to Jobling: The Necessity of Being 'Outside.'" *Semeia* 18 (1980): 51–53.

Yeats, William Butler. "The Second Coming." In *Collected Poems*. London: MacMillan & Co., 1967, 210–11.

Ziolkowski, Eric J. "The Bad Boys of Bethel: Origin and Development of a Sacrilegious Type." *History of Religions* 30 (1991): 331–58.